North American
Desert Sheep Hunting

Leonard Hansen

TC
TURNKEY
COMMUNICATIONS

ISBN 978-0-9893007-5-9 (hard cover)

First edition, 2024

Published by TurnKey Communications
Oklahoma City, Oklahoma
www.turnkeycommo.com
info@turnkeycommo.com

Autographed editions of this book can be purchased at:

oklahomabooksonline.com/leonard-hansen

Bulk purchases at discounts are available in the U.S. for corporations, institutions, and other organizations. For more information, please contact the publisher at: info@turnkeycommo.com or Leonard Hansen at: hansenproperty@yahoo.com

10 9 8 7 6 5 4 3 2 1

To the public officials, game managers,
wildlife biologists, wild sheep organizations,
and hunters who have contributed to the
ongoing recovery of North American
bighorn sheep

———————————

CONTENTS

Preface, vii

PREFACE

HAVING TAKEN THE FIRST THREE of the four wild sheep species needed to qualify for a Grand Slam of North American Wild Sheep, I headed back to the Big Bend region of southwest Texas in fall 2011. Twice before over the previous eleven months I had made this same trip and driven back to my home in Oklahoma City disappointed with the result. I had a Dall, Stone, and Rocky Mountain ram, but still needed the desert bighorn to complete the Slam.

The third trip was a charm. Shooting from the Mexican side of the Rio Grande, I downed a nice specimen on a rocky cliff on U.S. soil—an unusual but perfectly legal "international shot." I had my Grand Slam and my first subspecies of desert bighorn ram, an *Ovis canadensis mexicana.*

And I was hooked on hunting these skittish, inaccessible creatures. I loved the physical challenge of hunting desert bighorns and the beauty of their exotic habitat in the arid, rocky expanses of the American Southwest and northwestern Mexico. I booked more of these rewarding adventures.

Yet looking back, harvesting my first desert ram didn't have to be so troublesome and expensive. But I didn't know at that time that I could have had a knowledgeable biologist out of the Texas Parks and Wildlife office guide me on one of these hunts. That's just one of the lessons I learned as I spent the next eight years on another personal "grand slam" quest—the generally accepted four subspecies of desert bighorn sheep.

Which brings me to the primary motivation for writing this book. I want to provide a reliable source of information and inspiration to those hunters out there who yearn to have a handsome desert ram trophy gracing their game room. Due to the scarcity of permits and ruggedness of habitat, this quest will be difficult enough even if armed with a reliable guidebook of where and how to hunt these intriguing subspecies of *Ovis canadensis*. But this book, I hope, will take some of the head-scratching out of this and enhance the thrill of this outdoor adventure.

The first chapter of this book provides information on each of the four widely accepted subspecies of desert bighorn sheep—*nelsoni, mexicana, weemsi* and *cremnobates*. How these ecologic classifications evolved is an interesting story in itself. Recognizing the physical traits and understanding the behaviors of these sheep will be important to both a hunter of these animals or to anyone just wanting to appreciate these exotic critters in the outdoors.

The next several chapters will be narratives of my desert bighorn hunts between 2010 and 2019. I hope these accounts will give the full flavor of what you are likely to encounter on these quests. These hunting chapters will include photos and maps to provide as much information as possible. Besides useful information from these experiences, I hope to provide some inspiration for the readers' own exploits.

Chapter 6 tells where in the United States and Mexico to find these sheep. Fortunately, a public and private effort to promote the numbers of these sheep has been paying off in the last several decades. Desert bighorns have been introduced in new areas, and those in established ranges are being better conserved by wildlife officials and private landholders to ensure bigger, healthier herds. Their populations have stabilized and even increased significantly.

With the last chapter of this book, I intend to provide a service both to the hunters of desert bighorn and the wildlife officials who regulate the hunting of these animals and work to conserve their populations. Hunting regulations vary from state to state, of course, so this book intends to give sheep hunters a good start to understanding and complying with these laws. This chapter will provide an overview of each state's laws for hunting desert ram, including the application process and cost of obtaining a tag-permit for a sheep.

I've sought and obtained these tags numerous times over the years, so I this overview will take some of the mystery out of this often-difficult process. A listing of state offices is included in this last chapter to help hunters obtain more detailed information about a particular state's permitting, hunting regulations, and current sheep populations.

Much of what a sheep hunter needs to know about these quests is available on the websites of the various states' wildlife departments. I've tried to give some of the key links at each of these online sites to get a hunter off to a good start in completing the process of planning, applying for, and completing a desert sheep hunt.

While this book is unashamedly written for hunters of desert bighorn rams, other groups should find this information worthwhile. Wildlife officials might be able to gain a better perspective of the hunters they work with daily. Additionally, wildlife photographers and outdoor enthusiasts can find locations for viewing these magnificent desert animals.

Information in this book about the history, habitat, characteristics and hunting of desert sheep draws heavily on several respected works long in print: James Clark's *The Great Arc of the Wild Sheep* (1964), Jack O'Connor's *Sheep and Sheep Hunting* (1974), editors Gale Monson and Lowell Sumner's *The Desert Bighorn: Its Life, History, Ecology and Management* (1980), and Lance Stapleton's *A Reference Manual for Hunting North American Sheep* (1991). With the most recent of the above classics now more than thirty years old, I also used two more recent sources, Mark Jorgensen's *Desert Bighorn Sheep: Wilderness Icon* (2015) and Dale Toweill and Valerius Geist's *Return of Royalty* (1999). Jorgensen's fine work provides both scholarly information and eye-popping photographs of desert bighorns and the striking landscapes they inhabit. Toweill and Geist's book celebrates and documents the success of wild game management's recovery of wild sheep populations in the closing decades of the last century.

Standing on the shoulders of these past works and written from a hunter's perspective, *North American Desert Sheep Hunting* provides a more up-to-date resource for those who seek these regal creatures in their austere, desert habitat.

Leonard Hansen
Oklahoma City, Oklahoma, Fall 2024

CHAPTER 1

Desert Bighorn Sheep: An Overview

Adapted to a mountainous desert environment with little or no permanent standing water, the desert bighorn sheep of North America—actually all the continent's bighorn sheep— descended from the wild sheep of central Asia. As any student of North American wild sheep has read, Asian sheep are theorized to have crossed the well-traveled Bering Sea land bridge to present-day Alaska during the peak glacial period of the ice ages.

With so much of the waters of the oceans frozen in the massive glaciers covering the earth's surface, the lowered sea levels exposed areas in previously shallow waters. Thus, more than ten thousand years or so back, this allowed temporary land crossings in parts of the earth's surface like the floors of the Bering Sea.

As climate, habitat and time worked to adapt these massively horned ungulates to the North American continent, the northern Dall group of thinhorn sheep, *Ovis dalli*, evolved along with their relatives to the south, the American or Rocky Mountain group of bighorn sheep, *Ovis canadensis*. The Dall clung to the cold, snowy regions of Alaska and northwestern Canada. Their snowbird cousins spread southward down the mountainous landscapes of western North America.

Prior to the 19th century, the Rocky Mountain bighorn domain ranged from western Canada southward through the western United States and northwestern Mexico, and as far east as the western Dakotas and Oklahoma Panhandle. Western settlement in the United States greatly reduced the numbers and range of these bighorns, with the larger populations of the southern bighorns currently found only in the most remote mountainous and arid parts of their formerly expansive territory.

Climate, habitat and time led to variances in the southernmost *Ovis canadensis* species. The emerging subspecies of desert dwellers, the southernmost of the Rocky Mountain bighorn, often overlap and generally frustrate the taxonomical abilities of even the most learned naturalists. By the 1980s a shaky consensus had emerged for classifying desert bighorn sheep in four generally accepted subspecies. As stated earlier in the preface, the four desert subspecies, or races, for purposes of this book are the Nelson bighorn (*Ovis canadensis nelsoni*), Mexican bighorn (*Ovis canadensis mexicana*), Peninsular bighorn (*Ovis canadensis cremnobates*), and Weems bighorn (*Ovis canadensis weemsi*).

Monson and Sumner's 1980 book, *Desert Bighorn: Its Life, History, Ecology and Management*, appears to be among the first major works about North American wild sheep that clearly defines these four races of desert bighorn as "ecologic entities." The authors declare desert sheep in North America to be "any bighorn living under relatively arid desert conditions." These four subspecies were also accepted in a renowned U.S. Fish and Wildlife Service report, "Desert Bighorn Sheep: A Guide to Selected Management Practices," in 1988. With most of these desert sheep on federal lands of the U.S. Southwest, this widely read special report addressed concerns for the management and conservation of these threatened animals.

These classifications notwithstanding, the discerning outdoorsman always keeps in mind the unruliness of Mother Nature. A pristine racial classification for desert bighorn sheep is impossible, so we are left with these generally accepted subspecies based largely on their ecology. Realizing these taxonomic limitations, we can still recognize and appreciate the distinctions between these wild inhabitants of generally inhospitable desert terrain adjoining low, rugged mountain ranges and rocky hillsides.

From their cooler, wetter environment in the north, the Rocky Mountain group of bighorn sheep (*Ovis canadensis*) spread southward down the mountainous landscapes of western North America.

Moreover, students and hunters of the desert bighorn should appreciate just how much the dry, inhospitable habitat of these four races of desert dwellers determine to some degree their physical appearance and to a larger degree their ecologic classification. Just like the races of the peoples of the earth, the *homo sapiens*, the races of desert bighorns display physical characteristics determined by and adapted to their environment. As the lean bodies of the Australian aborigines in the Outback reflected their limited diets and enhanced their hunter-gatherer abilities, so has the desert sheep's smaller body size been shaped by the less favorable forage in its harsh environment. Even the considerable wear shown on the corrugations of the horns of desert sheep partly results from their habit of smashing open local cacti for hydration and nutrition.

3

North American Desert Sheep Hunting

Although the home ranges of desert bighorn sheep are in the arid desert regions of western North America, their preferred habitat is neither flat nor readily accessible. Hunters of these desert nomads should be prepared to cross rugged terrain with steeply pitched ascents and descents.

Although we call these ungulates of the arid regions of North America desert sheep, these wary animals live mainly in and around rugged, elevated terrain that discourages access by predators and provides an escape route when threatened. Rough and rocky canyons, steep cliffsides, and rocky ascents characterize the broken landscape within the warm, dry homelands of desert bighorn sheep. As hunters of these sheep can attest, pursuit of this game usually requires more up-and-down scrambling than hiking across flat, desert landscape.

Similarities in their habitat aside, the subspecies classification of the desert bighorn also depends, often arbitrarily, on their geographic location in the arid U.S. Southwest and northwestern Mexico. As James Clark succinctly describes the dilemma in classifying desert bighorn in his widely read *Great Arc of the Wild Sheep*, "we are reminded that unless we can say exactly where a particular sheep was taken, there is some difficulty in telling just what sheep it may be."

Desert Sheep Past and Present

One of the first written records of desert bighorn sightings is from the journey of the Spanish explorer Francisco Vázquez de Coronado, who reported on these sheep while futilely searching for the legendary city of gold across present-day southwest United States. Prone to exaggeration like other explorers of the age, Coronado described seeing "some sheep as big as a Horse, with very large horns and little tails."

More accurately, Jesuit missionaries working on the Baja California peninsula in 1697 wrote of seeing mountain sheep "as large as a Calf of one or two years old: Its Head is much like that of a Stag: and its Horns, which are very large, like those of a Ram: Its Tail and Hair are speckled...." A later Spanish missionary in California gave a similar description and even provided a drawing, likely the first published picture of the desert bighorn of North America.

None of this would have been news to the native inhabitants of the region. Paintings and petroglyphs of these sheep by North American inhabitants from many centuries past are common. These depictions can still be seen in stone blinds within sprawling Inyo County of southeastern California, where these ancient ones crouched in hiding for these sheep. Similar blinds can be seen in steep-walled canyons of arid lands in other states of the American Southwest. Biding their time in these shelters while awaiting prey, these native North Americans often painted or scratched crude depictions of bighorns on the rock walls. These pictographs and petroglyphs of wild bighorn sheep can be found as far east as the Oklahoma Panhandle.

The desert bighorn was a welcome addition to the starvation diet of these desert tribesmen, but their efforts with spear and bow only minimally threatened these sheep populations. The flood of American settlers from the east throughout the 19th century, however, nearly reduced these herds to extinction. Hunting for food and sport, diseases from domestic livestock, and reductions in forage and habitat all took a mighty toll.

Wildlife officials estimate current populations of bighorn sheep in the western United States at about 5 percent of the numbers as recently as two centuries ago. Fortunately, the shy creatures are not as imperiled as they were late in the last century. Populations of Rocky Mountain bighorns and desert subspecies have been successfully restored in areas of the United States and Mexico, thanks to the efforts of hunting and conservation groups, state and federal wildlife agencies, private landowners, and hunters themselves.

An estimate in Marc Jorgensen's 2015 *Desert Bighorn Sheep: Wilderness Icon* put the number of desert bighorn in North America at around 31,000. Several thousand more are being raised in fenced areas, mostly in Mexico. Using recent publications and various states' wildlife websites, I would estimate current populations of desert wild sheep at nearing 35,000.

I have personally seen how conservation and restoration efforts pay off. The Black Gap Wildlife Management Area was started by the Texas Parks and Wildlife Department in 1948, and a growing population of desert sheep (*Ovis canadensis mexicana*) has been restored

on these 100,000 acres bordering Big Bend National Park on the northeast. With the population of sheep in West Texas estimated near zero in 1960, current herds are quite significant. Area ranchers contribute to these conservation efforts with most benefiting

Ancient pictographs in the Oklahoma Panhandle told of the area's desert bighorn, and this photo confirms their tentative return to these rocky homelands near the Colorado border.

from regulated sales of permits to hunters. My first desert bighorn was taken with a purchased permit on a private ranch just north of Black Gap. (More on that later.)

Physical Characteristics and Senses

Desert bighorn sheep differ from their Rocky Mountain bighorn cousins primarily in size and coloration—and of course, location. It's important to include location as a distinguishing characteristic because, as emphasized above, it is sometimes the only discernible difference between the Rocky Mountain bighorn and the desert bighorn subspecies. To that point, in Clark's seminal work on wild sheep he considers the desert sheep that inhabit the rugged, arid regions of the American Southwest and northwestern Mexico as an arbitrary term for Rocky Mountain sheep. Likewise, he considers just as arbitrary the classifications for the subspecies of desert sheep, noting their variance as mostly in their locations.

Yet that very location that often arbitrarily determines the classification of desert sheep undeniably affects their physical characteristics, beginning with body mass. As a rule, desert sheep are noticeably smaller than other Rocky Mountain bighorns, but with a stocky build similar to mule deer. While exceptions can always be found, the reduced calories and minerals in desert forage almost invariably limit their body size. Less affected by this reduced diet, the horns on a desert bighorn ram often appear massive. This is usually just an illusion though, as these horns are out of proportion to the thinner necks and smaller bodies.

Clark favorably compares the body size of desert sheep to that of their northern cousins, the Dall sheep in Alaska and northwestern Canada, that also struggle finding good forage. He considers a weight of 180 to 200 pounds as large for a desert ram. By his standard, an average bighorn male in arid terrain would weigh in at around 155 to 175 pounds.

In their 1980 book, *Desert Bighorn*, Monson and Summers put an average desert bighorn at 160 pounds, slightly smaller than Clark's estimate but in the same ballpark. Stapleton's reference manual for desert sheep provides a slightly more generous assessment of around 170-175 pounds for an average mature ram.

North American Desert Sheep Hunting

As Monson and Sumner's book points out, weight of these rams varies considerably by time of year. Early summer seems to be the peak of body mass and mid-winter the nadir. This obviously correlates with availability of forage. Breeding season is another time-of-year factor in body weight for rams. The rut period for these sheep ranges from late summer to end of fall, and a ram will sometimes forego regular meals in pursuit of a winsome ewe. It should also be noted that the rut period for desert sheep extends over a greater number of months than that of their northern kin.

Sources vary on the shoulder height of adult desert bighorn, with Monson and Sumner giving a range of 30 to 39 inches. Clark ranges shoulder height from 36 to 40 inches. Averaging these two sources gives a height for the desert ram comparable to the Dall.

Most sources agree that the pelage of desert bighorns is generally lighter hued than that of their Rocky Mountain kin. No doubt owing to climate, the pelage of the desert dwellers is also thinner than the bighorn of cooler climes. Clark notes that the Nelson sheep (*Ovis canadensis nelsoni*) has the lightest coat of all the desert sheep.

The pelage of desert bighorn sheep is generally lighter in hue than their Rocky Mountain kin, a consequence of the relentless desert sunlight.

Monson and Sumner's work remarks more on the wide variety of coloration for all desert sheep, and even the wide range of color changes throughout the seasons. Some have observed a more distinctive white rump patch in the southern sheep, but that may be too broad a characterization. There are some subtle color distinctions among the four subspecies of desert bighorns, and this will be discussed below specific to each.

Despite the general consensus of the desert sheep's paler pelage, exceptions are as common as the darker and lighter variations of Rocky Mountain sheep. Jack O'Connor writes that the darkest wild sheep he ever saw was a desert bighorn ram in the San Francisco Mountains of Sonora. The black hair on its neck was so dark that its horns appeared almost yellow in contrast. The legendary sheep hunter discounts significant color distinctions between the desert bighorn and Rocky Mountain sheep, stating that these distinctions result more from age, with older rams generally darker than younger rams.

There is no strong consensus in color distinction for desert sheep. Suffice it to say that compared with other species of North American wild sheep, the southernmost *Ovis canadensis* usually have a somewhat lighter-colored pelage, which is almost always thinner. Testimony to the contrary is almost always anecdotal.

The horns of desert rams compare favorably with the Rocky Mountain rams, but again, they often appear larger on the hoof due to the smaller body size. Monson and Sumner have good data on horn size of the desert sheep, giving an average range of 30 to 40 inches on the outside curl for males, and 10 to 13 inches for the ewes. Basal circumference for mature rams averages around 12 inches but may range up to 14.5 inches.

The Boone and Crockett score of 205 1/8 points for a desert bighorn trophy has stood since first recorded in 1946. This prize was taken by a native meat hunter in Baja California in 1941. Second place is also from a Baja California ram, and seven of the ten largest desert ram trophies came from this same Mexican state at the time of Monson and Sumner's book publication in 1980.

Clark notes the tighter curl in the horns of the desert sheep and the smaller corrugations. He also remarks on the considerable wear on these horns, which he says may result not only from their battles during mating season but also from their use smashing open the cacti prevalent in the desert areas. Thus the brooming and scarring on the horn tips so common on seasoned rams of all North American wild sheep appears more pronounced in the desert species.

Monson and Sumner's work posits a "stress theory" for the more prominent brooming common to the desert ram. Rams in the Desert National Wildlife Refuge north of Las Vegas, Nevada, have been observed butting rocks and posts as well as other bighorn and cacti. This may be a means of taking out their frustrations under stress. So with the harsher living conditions in the arid landscapes, these sheep could be projecting their angst on any available target—other rams, cacti, rocks, posts. Hard to know, but an interesting theory.

Important to hunters and observers of desert bighorn, these animals' senses of sight, hearing and smell are a frequent topic of discussion. Most of this information, unfortunately, is anecdotal and rarely from unbiased observations over a significant period of time. But a general consensus of the acuity of desert sheep's eyes, ears and noses has emerged that should be helpful to anyone hoping to get closer to these skittish critters.

Like all bighorn sheep, desert bighorn have an extremely well-developed sense of sight to protect against predators. This keen eyesight is their primary early warning system. Desert sheep authority R. E. Welles succinctly made the case for their excellent visual acuity some 65 years ago. "The fact that they have good vision is too well known to warrant general discussion," he wrote seemingly to close any debate. "We have seen ample proof of this in distant vision and in close vision associated with the incredible surefootedness of the species."

Stalkers of these sheep can expect to be spotted at a distance of one mile. At this distance the presence of an intruder will usually cause nervousness, at a minimum. Especially wary bighorn may even start to drift away. This kind of vision in any game calls for good binoculars or a spotting scope coupled with a patient, carefully planned stalk.

Desert sheep hunters must also take into account these ruminants' keen sense of smell. Even when completely concealed and at

distances as much as 400 yards, hunters have reported sheep react-
ing to wind shifts in their direction. Conversely, concealed hunters
downwind of these sheep have reported getting within 100 yards
without reaction. Those distances are probably good rules of thumb
in the field. Concealed but upwind of sheep, expect a reaction as
distant as 400 yards; concealed but downwind, you're likely safe up
to 100 yards.

The desert sheep's hearing ability is the only break a hunter might
get. They certainly have no hearing problems, but most observers
report their hearing to be about the same as humans. So a whisper
at 75 to 100 yards should be safe. On the other hand, the clang of a
metal canteen dropped on a rock may carry several hundred yards
on a still morning—easily discerned by the ear of a wary ram.

Interestingly, research shows that these sheep learn to differenti-
ate between sounds that might mean danger—including any sound
that is unfamiliar—versus sounds that are usually safe. Volume
doesn't seem to matter. Sheep subjected to sonic booms eventually
show no reaction. But don't expect them to confuse a sonic boom
with a rifle boom.

Feeding Hydrating and Daily Movement

Most daily activities of all wild sheep are governed by their quest
for nutrition and hydration, but probably more so for desert sheep
owing to the scarcity of both in their habitat. This same scarcity of
forage in arid areas also makes desert sheep less particular about
their diets. Monson and Sumner's book is chock-full of research on
the eating and drinking habits of desert sheep, so most of this information comes from their fine work.

Of the three primary types of forage for these ruminants—
grasses, browse (including cacti), and forbs (herbaceous flowering
plants)—most North American wild sheep prefer grasses. This gen-
eralization is less valid for the desert bighorn, likely because of their
forced adaptation to a variety of edibles.

The more northern desert sheep consume grasses for most of
their nutrition. In the southern regions they rely more on browse and
forbs. Whether this is from preference or necessity has not been de-
finitively determined, but some researchers lean more to necessity.

More certainly out of necessity, desert sheep in the southern regions are not averse to consuming this forage in a desiccated state.

Additionally, research shows that a feeding ground for desert bighorn is usually within a six-mile radius of a permanent or extremely reliable water source. And since plant life can get scarce during certain times of year in a dry, hot climate, desert sheep usually range over a wider area. These animals will thus find a number of locations to forage to satisfy their need for a proximate water source.

With the wide variety of the kinds and availability of forage for the desert bighorn, specific statements about dietary habits are difficult. Suffice it to say that these sheep are less particular about what

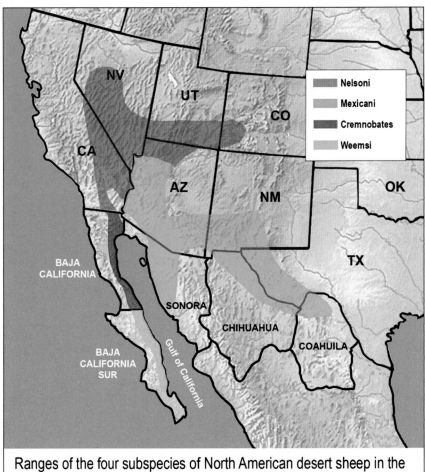

Ranges of the four subspecies of North American desert sheep in the United States and Mexico.

they eat, as forage can be scarce in a hot, dry habitat. Cacti and dried-up plants are on the menu.

A minimal amount of surface water must be available at all times to maintain a healthy sheep herd, although desert sheep in the Sonoran Desert seem to be an exception. The lack of a reliable water supply is the single-greatest limiting factor on populations of desert bighorn. This same scarcity of water in desert areas also limits forage for these sheep, so the arid conditions wield a two-edged sword on these ungulates.

The water lost by desert sheep in urine, feces, respiration and evaporation must be replaced to prevent dehydration. They rely on three sources for this—surface water, preformed moisture in forage, and metabolic hydration (internal generation)—to maintain this balance of inflow and outflow.

Surface water plays the major role, and these sheep have adapted physiologically to make the most of it. A healthy ram can guzzle over one-fifth of his body weight in water in one visit to a water hole. So a 180-pound bighorn can easily trot away with between four and five gallons taken in from a single "happy hour"—but in far less than 60 minutes. Desert bighorns have been observed gulping a gallon of water in less than 90 seconds. This "chugging speed" is likely a survival adaptation for this necessary, but dangerous, activity. Exposed and distracted while hydrating, this is usually the most vulnerable time for wild sheep.

Water requirements for desert sheep and locations of sources vary according to season. Naturally, they need more water during periods of high temperatures. During the heat of summer, these bighorns drink daily when a source is available. They can, however, go without drinking water for about a week during hot periods. Again, the camel-like Sonoran sheep are an exception.

From late fall through early spring, desert sheep in general have little need for a source of standing water. They lose far less moisture through respiration and evaporation, and the water content of their forage is usually higher. Their third source of water, metabolic hydration, also supplies more of their overall need during these cooler months. While this internal process of breaking down fats, carbohydrates and protein produces only a fraction of the water needed during the summer months, this same small amount is significant during cooler weather.

Desert sheep are fortunate if they have a nearby spring or pond during hot periods, and if so, they capitalize on this source with daily visits. But in many desert areas, springs and ponds dry up in the heat of summer, and the bighorn rely on generally reliable potholes in rocks and the more permanent *tinajas* (potholes that rarely or never dry up). With most desert sheep preferring to drink water on a daily basis during summer, their habitat corresponds with the availability of a regular water source. During dry periods in hot months when their usual sources give out, bighorns reestablish themselves in a different area.

In summary of their drinking habits, during the heat of summer, these sheep establish—or reestablish—in areas within a half-dozen miles or less from perennial water. In the cooler months with lower water requirements, these bighorns are prone to "drift" and expand their range. So in these cooler weather periods, the range of wild sheep becomes less predictable, making them harder to find.

Outside their never-ending quest for water and forage, the daily movement of desert bighorn and all their northern relatives can be

The "chugging speed" of some desert sheep has been documented at a gallon of water in less than 90 seconds.

unpredictable, as anyone who has hunted this wild game can attest. But a general pattern can be relied on. They usually rise at dawn and feed for a period of one to three hours. This is followed by a one- to three-hour rest period when they bed down. This feeding and resting alternates throughout the day, and ends with a climb to higher ground and a bedding for the night at dusk.

More specifically but less reliably, in cooler periods of the year the day beds are most likely to be found on the southern slopes of hills or mountains. In hotter weather, the day beds are often in the shade of trees or rocks. Bighorn will often use the same beds during the day and at night.

Geographic Distribution of Desert Sheep

The southernmost Rocky Mountain bighorn herds in the United States—the four subspecies of desert bighorns—are almost all found in southern California, across Nevada, southern Utah, western and southern Arizona, southwestern New Mexico, and now in far west Texas. In Mexico, these desert sheep are located on the eastern coast of the California peninsula—in the Mexican states of Baja California and Baja California Sur—in west-central Sonora, and in smaller numbers just south of the New Mexico-Texas borders in northern areas of Chihuahua and Coahuila. (see map nearby) Current estimates of wild desert bighorn sheep in North American are around 35,000 of these hardy survivors.

The areas on the nearby map closely follow those of Jorgensen's 2015 map for desert bighorn and that of the 1988 U.S. Fish and Wildlife report, "Desert Bighorn Sheep: A Guide to Selected Management Practices." As stated earlier, Mother Nature can be a little unruly, so I have tamed her somewhat with a firm designation of the four subspecies of desert bighorn based primarily on geography.

Nelson Sheep (*Ovis canadensis nelsoni*)

The Nelson wild sheep range from southeastern California, throughout Nevada, southern Utah, and northwestern Arizona. Their southeastern boundary is the Colorado River.

In the last few decades, Nevada has surpassed Arizona as the U.S. state with the most Nelson bighorn. In fact, state wildlife officials claim the most bighorn sheep of any state in the lower 48. From a few desert herds totaling less than 2,000 in 1980, the state's trapping and transplanting program increased these numbers five-fold to nearly 10,000 by 2018. Many of the Nelsons in northwest Nevada have been relocated from California.

About 5,000 Nelson sheep occupy the harsh, arid areas of southeastern California, mostly in and around the Mojave Desert. Next door in Arizona, only the vast Coconino County in the northwestern corner holds sizable numbers of the Nelsons, mainly in and around the Grand Canyon. Southern Utah has recently seen a large rebound in desert sheep that now rival the herds of southeastern California. Southwestern Colorado also has seen a recent surge in Nelson sheep with numbers now around 500.

Most of the best source books on desert bighorn define their ranges—always in a desert environment with low, rugged mountains or hills—but make little effort to describe distinguishing characteristics among the four subspecies, considering them almost physically indistinguishable. The renowned James Clark, however, does attempt to make physical distinctions.

Clark notes that the Nelson sheep are among the smaller desert sheep, with shoulder height rarely exceeding 38 inches. He describes their horns as comparable to their Rocky Mountain bighorn cousins, but "generally lighter and slightly flaring." He also describes the horns as "light-reddish-yellow" with medium corrugations. The Nelson's pelage is among the lightest of the desert sheep, and Clark describes it as usually "light-buff with a little deeper reddish-yellow tinge on the neck and shoulders with a more grayish tinge on the under parts." The ears are smaller than the other desert sheep, and closer to that of Rocky Mountain bighorn.

Mexican Sheep (*Ovis canadensis mexicana*)

The Mexican wild sheep had the largest population of the four desert bighorn subspecies until being surpassed by the Nelsons in the last decade or so. Combining their large numbers in Arizona and the Mexican state of Sonora with the those in the sprawling range across the southwestern U.S. border provides an estimated 13,000 of these desert sheep, the southernmost in the United States.

Arizona's estimated 4,500 with Sonora's 3,700 (which includes the 350 on Tiburon Island) made up more than half of the Mexican race of desert sheep in 2023. But in almost every range of this vast, arid region, these *mexicana* populations have increased over the last few decades. Texas is a prime example of the conservation and restoration efforts driving these increases. With a negligible population of Mexican sheep in the early 1950s, the restocking efforts in Texas have raised these numbers to around 1,500 sheep in eleven free-ranging herds by 2023.

Monson and Sumner's book has most of the desert bighorn in Arizona concentrated in Yuma County in the state's southwestern corner. The low, harsh mountains in Yuma County provide an excellent habitat for these sheep. The large county contains roughly twenty-five small mountain ranges supporting these bighorns.

Clark designates all desert sheep east of the Colorado River as of the Mexican variety, calling the river an "effective barrier" to desert sheep living on either side of these waters. This distinction is similar to that of the Peace River in Canada marking the southern boundary of Stone sheep. For this book, I am using Clark's Colorado River demarcation line for the Mexican sheep in the United States.

Beyond geographic distinctions, Clark rates the Mexican sheep as among the largest of the desert bighorns. A particularly distinguishing characteristic of this race of sheep are the long, pointed ears, which Clark said may be twice the length of the Rocky Mountain bighorns of Canada.

Clark describes the horns of the Mexican as "pale yellow superimposed with a reddish brown," a color that he speculates comes from the soil and oxidized saps from vegetation. From my own experiences in Sonora, the reddish-brown horns of the Mexican sheep in Sonora are ascribed to their rubbing on pine trees and evergreens in the higher elevations. This darker shade of horn has promoted the name "Sonoran darkhorn" as a descriptor for these sheep.

Besides their darker horns, the Mexican sheep in Sonora are renowned for their ability to survive with little or no water for long periods. Jack O'Connor writes of a Sonoran outfitter telling him these sheep could get by without standing water indefinitely, getting all the hydration they needed from vegetation dew and from moisture in cacti and other forage. This is likely an exaggeration, but certainly the Sonoran has adapted to the arid conditions better than most desert sheep. Authoritative sources report these camel-like Sonoran sheep can go for up to a month in hot weather without a source of standing water. This is opposed to about a week for other desert sheep in the summer heat.

According to Clark, the body color of Mexican sheep is generally darker than the other desert sheep. He calls it "dark brown, darkest on throat, legs and tail." Clark's description gibes closely with the Mexican I took in Sonora in 2014—dark horns and reddish-brown body. The very first *mexicani* I took near Big Bend National Park in 2011 had similar body color as the Sonoran but the horns were not as dark. Clark distinguishes the body color of the Mexicans as having more of a reddish tint as opposed to the Nelson with its tannish tint.

Peninsular Sheep (*Ovis canadensis cremnobates*)

Clark's general name for the *cremnobates* sub specie of Rocky

Mountain bighorn sheep was "lower California bighorn," which he described as "rather large, pale sheep, perhaps the palest of all, with massive horns and large ears." Clark's use of the term "lower California" refers to the region in

The almost chocolate-colored pelage of this Sonoran darkhorn ram taken by the author attests to the color variations of the desert sheep.

Mexico just south of the U.S. state of California—not to the lower region of the Baja peninsula. The name Peninsular bighorn eventually became common for these sheep.

The oversized horns of this subspecies were well known even before Clark's writing about them in 1964. The record trophy taken in the 1940s on the southern end of the Sierra San Pedro Martir Mountains still stands today, as well as a number of top-10 trophies from this state on the Baja.

Although most of the top desert bighorn trophies were taken in the northern Baja peninsula, since 1993 wild sheep hunting has been banned in the Mexican state of Baja California—the northern region of the peninsula. Conservation efforts and a strong anti-hunting attitude in the state have continued to work against legalized sheep hunts.

An extensive analysis of data from a 2010 survey of these desert sheep produced an estimate of around 2,500 bighorns inhabiting the remote mountain ranges of the state. Officials concluded that the population has stabilized at these numbers for the previous thirty years or so.

For hunters wanting a *cremnobates* specimen or needing one to complete a "desert bighorn slam," a few of these sheep have either migrated or been relocated into Baja California Sur—the southern region of the peninsula. Hunts exclusively for these immigrant bighorns can be arranged in this state to the south of Baja California and better known for its population of Weems wild sheep.

Weems Sheep (*Ovis canadensis weemsi*)

Although Jesuit missionaries in the southern Baja California peninsula reported seeing these bighorn sheep as far back as the 17th century, these animals remained mysterious until the 1930s when "discovered" by F. Carrington Weems. A financial specialist for J. P. Morgan and a noted big game hunter, in 1936 Weems led an expedition into the Mexican territory that later became Baja California Sur.

Seeing the large, dark bighorns, Weems and a mammalogist from the Smithsonian Institute, E. A. Goldman, discerned enough differences in these ungulates to declare a new subspecies, *Ovis canadensis weemsi*, immodestly named after the expedition leader. Found in the Sierra de la Giganta mountain range that parallels the eastern coastline of the peninsula, Goldman's description of the new subspecies was: "Large size—color dark for a desert subspecies...Closely allied to *O. c. cremnobates,* size similar, but pelage shorter—color usually darker, varying to very dark brown more or less distinctively mixed with black."

Weems's team reported the skull size larger and heavier than Nelson sheep and with "massive widely spreading horns of rams [that] approach those of *cremnobates.*" In a follow-up to this decades later, Clark said the Weems sheep might be the largest of the desert bighorns. He based this on the measurements he took of the large skulls in a number of Weems specimens.

From the town of Loreto in the north to Cabo San Lucas at the southern tip of the peninsula, Weems sheep live in the mountainous desert landscape with black soils and ample drinking water from frequent rainfalls. Thick tropical vegetation grows among the pale blanco and palo verde trees. Organ pipe and prickly pear cactus thrive. With most of the sheep in the mountain ranges on the east side of the peninsula, visitors are treated to gorgeous views of the Gulf of California (also called Sea of Cortez), which separates the peninsula from mainland Mexico.

Even with evidence of the Weems's similar horn size to its cousin just to the north, most of the record trophies remain from hunts in Baja California and not Baja California Sur. This could be attributed to more hunting on the north end of the peninsula throughout the last century. The Mexican territory on the southern end of the peninsula didn't become the state of Baja California Sur until 1974. So the region was a remote, somewhat wild-and-woolly place throughout most of the twentieth century. Only the bolder sheep hunters dared to go.

The fewer numbers of desert bighorn on the southern end of the peninsula may also explain the lack of record trophies from B. C. Sur. The relatively small population of around 350 Weems sheep has remained stable for some time. Their major threat is not from hunters but livestock diseases.

THE FINAL CHAPTERS of this book provide information on

where desert sheep can be found and how the layman hunter can navigate the regulatory maize to pursue these prized game animals. Meantime, some of my actual experiences hunting these desert denizens are chronicled in the next several chapters.

By sharing these personal accounts, I hope to provide you with a little inspiration and direction to enhance your pursuit of one of these big-game icons.

CHAPTER 2

Mexicana Hunts in Big Bend Country
(2010-2011)

Returning from a successful Rocky Mountain bighorn hunt in Wyoming in October 2010, I received an email about a permit to hunt a desert bighorn ram just east of Big Bend National Park in west Texas. The email was sent to members of the Oklahoma City chapter of Safari Club from a member of another chapter in Fort Worth, Texas. This Texan had a cousin with a big ranch southeast of Marathon, Texas. Upon hearing that I had taken the Rocky Mountain bighorn ram in Wyoming, the president of our chapter emailed to urge my consideration of this desert bighorn opportunity.

I was definitely interested. Taking the Rocky ram had started the wheels turning in my head. I had gone to Alaska in 2003 and 2004 to take a Dall sheep to enhance my fairly extensive collection of Alaskan wild game. The successful 2004 Dall hunt in the Alaska Range fired me up about wild sheep hunting, and I wanted more of this challenging sport. I got some with a Rocky Mountain ewe hunt in 2006, and then more after getting drawn for a Rocky Mountain ram permit in Wyoming and bagging this regal animal in 2010. This put me halfway to a Grand Slam of North American Wild Sheep. The Slam had never been of major importance—I just loved hunting wild sheep. Still, having this hunting milestone within sight did energize me.

The ghostly Chisos Mountains are within Big Bend National Park in West Texas, near where I hunted my first desert bighorn sheep.

I moved quickly to secure the desert bighorn permit in Texas, negotiating a landowner tag (Texas has a landowner permit system) to hunt along the Rio Grande on Bear Canyon Ranch, a spread owned by members of the Rhodes family. I purchased the tag from family member Barry Crumrine. Although I paid a relatively low price, this was far more than any I had ever purchased for wild game. At the time, some desert bighorn hunters were paying more than $100,000 for those tags in Texas. With my permit secured, I was in position for the third leg of my Grand Slam. Taking a desert bighorn, however, would prove more challenging than I initially thought.

Only a week after my return from Wyoming, I was off to Texas on another sheep hunting adventure. One of my taxidermists, Mike Chain from Oklahoma City, and his Hispanic wife, Cocese, accompanied me to this Big Bend region of West Texas. Fluent in Spanish, Cocese had helped re-establish desert bighorn hunting years earlier in the area of northern Mexico around Big Bend National Park.

This restoration program in Mexico coincided with similar efforts in West Texas.

I was fortunate for any opportunity to hunt a desert ram in this area. In 2007, just three years before I purchased my tag, only twelve desert bighorn ram permits were issued in Texas the entire year. At that time twelve was the most ever for a single year. The state had been extremely conservative with these permits since it reinstated desert bighorn hunting in 1988. This approach is justified. These sheep faced extirpation in the mountain ranges of west Texas by the 1950s, having declined from an estimated population of around 1,500 in 1880.

Efforts to restore Texas wild sheep populations first began in the mid-1950s when sixteen desert bighorns from Arizona were stocked in the Black Gap Wildlife Management Area, just northeast of Big Bend National Park and abutting the area I would hunt on Bear Canyon Ranch. A cooperative effort by Texas Parks and Wildlife Department, Texas Bighorn Society, Wild Sheep Foundation, Dallas Safari Club, and private landowners had restored the desert bighorn population in Texas to around a thousand by 2010.

Pulling a borrowed ATV in a trailer, Mike, Cocese and I left Oklahoma City in late October for the Big Bend region of West Texas. We crossed the famed Pecos River and drove southwest toward the town of Alpine, the county seat of Brewster County. To verify our landowner permit, we checked in with a game warden at the Texas Parks and Wildlife office in Alpine.

I had called one of the game wardens at this office a few days earlier and asked him to describe the country I would be hunting. "Have you ever been to the Grand Canyon?" he asked. "Well, it's a lot like it."

I soon learned that the game warden's description was on the mark, although I would describe the canyonlands of the Rio Grande more as a mini-Grand Canyon. Over the ages, the Colorado River carved the vast Grand Canyon while the Rio Grande cut the smaller canyons of the Big Bend region, named after the river's semi-circular course on the southern border of West Texas. The daunting cliffs and slopes along the sides of the rivers in both these canyons make for tough hiking. The rivers themselves provide the fastest route

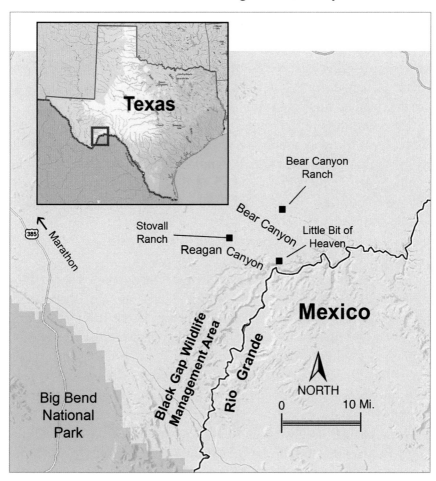

through these regions although white water in the Grand Canyon can make these boat rides plenty interesting. The waters of the Rio Grande flow more tamely and sometimes barely at all, especially in the dry years experienced in the decade or so before my visits.

We drove into Alpine at midday and found the Texas Parks and Wildlife office. This town of about six thousand is sandwiched between the Davis Mountains to the northwest and the Del Norte Mountains to the southeast. At an elevation of only 4,475 feet, the town's name is a stretch, but the mountains in the area provided a more interesting landscape than the many miles of flat, west Texas terrain than earlier that morning. The game warden signed off on my agreement letter with the Rhodes family, and this became my permit to hunt a Mexican desert ram (*Ovis canadensis mexicana*) on

Bear Canyon Ranch.

Our business in Alpine concluded, we proceeded from Alpine twenty-two miles east to Marathon, the nearest town to Bear Canyon Ranch. We skirted the western edge of the Glass Mountains as we approached this small west Texas town.

Even with less than five hundred residents, Marathon is the second-largest town in sparsely populated Brewster County. It serves as the jumping-off point to Big Bend National Park, and to both the southern and southeastern sections of the county. There are no other towns southeast of Marathon in the entire county, whose southern and southeastern borders bump against Mexico. And Brewster County is big—the largest county in Texas at nearly 6,200 square miles and six times the size of Rhode Island.

Marathon lies in the northern part of this huge county, some forty miles from the north entrance of Big Bend National Park, which sprawls southward another sixty miles or so to the Rio Grande and Mexico. The town has hosted the Marathon Marathon, a Boston Marathon qualifier, since around 2010. The late-October running event's motto is: "The hard part is getting there." Yes, the town is in a remote location. Its population usually doubles the weekend of the marathon.

We took U.S. Highway 385 out of Marathon, heading south toward Big Bend National Park. Passing a U.S. Border Patrol checkpoint, the guards were more interested in traffic opposite our direction. This federal facility serves as an interdiction point north of Big Bend National Park to staunch the flow of illegal immigrants and drugs from the south. To the southwest, the Santiago Mountains rose on the horizon. Directly south and farther ahead in the national park, the higher peaks of the exotic Chisos Mountains beckoned.

The wild beauty of Big Bend National Park exemplifies the exotic landscape of this region of Texas. As inviting as the park's distant Chisos peaks appeared, we were not going there. South of the federal checkpoint, we turned off the highway and onto a gravel road. The hunting lodge on Bear Canyon Ranch, where we would meet Barry Crumrine, lay along this gritty route and more than thirty miles to the east of our turnoff.

Slowing down on the unpaved road, we took a good look at this flat, desert terrain northeast of the more mountainous Big Bend National Park. We were driving in the northeast corner of the Chihuahuan Desert, an expansive eco-region that extends westward from the Pecos River across West Texas and southern New Mexico to southeast Arizona. It also extends deep into northern Mexico. With an area of 140,000 square miles, it is the third largest desert in the Western Hemisphere.

Daily high temperatures in lower elevations routinely break one hundred degrees from late spring to early fall. We planned to hunt in some of the lowest areas. Rainfall averages less than ten inches per year across this parched region. Despite its aridity, the region has a surprising diversity of plant species. Agave plants, yucca and prickly pear, creosote bushes, and the tall-stemmed ocotillo typify the flora of the Chihuahuan Desert. I would soon get a close look at some of this unusual growth.

We arrived at Bear Canyon Ranch in late afternoon. The hunting lodge was less than ten miles from the Rio Grande as the crow flies. The rough, winding jeep trail to the river, however, took about an hour and a half to drive. I found Barry Crumrine to be an affable Texan in his 60s. A couple of his friends were with him and would join our hunting party as sightseers. Barry showed us around the hunting lodge and gave us a short tour of the spread. Our sleeping arrangements at the lodge, considered our base camp, would be inside a secure metal building with indoor plumbing and electricity. This was about as upscale a base camp as I had experienced.

Early the next morning, Barry and his two companions loaded into one ATV and the Chains and I into another. With streaks of dawn spreading, we drove southeast from our lodge along the punishing jeep trail overlooking Bear Canyon. Our destination was a fishing camp beside the Rio Grande.

We stopped on a canyon overlook just as the sun broke the horizon. The harsh beauty of this terrain presented itself in all its glory. Sectioned off by limestone palisades of rimrock, a series of steeply sloping terraces spilled down the canyon walls. We stood on rocky, dry ground, surrounded by an array of sharp, spindly varieties of cactus, succulents and weeds. A local's pithy comment about the forbidding flora and fauna of the region proved accurate: "If it don't bite you, it will sure stick you." Desert sheep country, no doubt.

The temperature hovered in the mid-50s in the early morning, but it would soon be much warmer. The dry desert air holds little heat, allowing drastic temperature swings between night and day. With the sun lighting up the canyon below us, we began to glass in earnest. With six in our party, we could put a lot of eyes on the sheep, if there were any. The distant hillocks were barren of trees. Barry had earlier expressed concern that the sheep might be hard to find. He had not seen any around the canyon and the fishing camp in several weeks, but I reckoned that they lived in there somewhere. We just had to hunt them. After an hour or so, we gave up glassing the canyon and continued along the rocky jeep trail toward the fishing camp.

Our ATVs lurched alongside Bear Canyon for several more miles before the canyon walls of the river came into view. The Rio Grande flowed slowly in this section and made an impressive sight below the steep canyon walls. A large rock wall extended above the canyon's north rim to the east. I agreed with the game warden's assessment— a mini-Grand Canyon indeed.

Barry and his two friends' vehicle barely made it to a flat area above the fishing camp. Their ATV had developed a serious mechanical problem on the jolting trail, and the trio began working on this as soon as we stopped. Mike, Cocese and I walked up an overlook to glass for sheep on the slopes above the river.

Barry and his friends soon left in our ATV to retrieve a part for their broken vehicle while we positioned ourselves on an overlook of sheep trails leading to the river. These trails were about six hundred yards upriver from us and meandered down a steep, rocky slope to the water's edge. The river's shallow flow rippled over a sandbar at this point, so the sheep may have used this location for crossing. Several miles upriver, Nipple Mountain jutted upward. From its distinct outline on the horizon, it was obvious how this landmark got its name. We moved a little closer to the water and into the shadows of the canyon. We could see upriver for some distance, so this seemed a strategic position to hold for a while.

With the canyon growing darker in the late afternoon, we gave up finding sheep that day. The temperature hovered around one

Far from its chilly, boisterous headwaters in Colorado, the Rio Grande meanders sluggishly along the southern and eastern borders of Big Bend National Park, where we futilely searched for desert bighorn.

hundred degrees as we awaited Barry's return. When he arrived, he announced that a part to fix the broken ATV would not arrive for nearly a week, so Barry and his friends were leaving the area. Mike, Cocese and I would be hunting on our own in the coming days. But we knew the route to and from the fishing camp and wouldn't need the ranch owner to act as our guide.

We pounded and swerved along the jeep trail for close to an hour and a half before reaching our base camp at the metal hunting lodge. With most of the comforts of home in the well-stocked lodge, the Chains and I made the most of our evening. We cooked over the rustic grill and sat outdoors for hours in the desert night. I had only passing concern over not seeing any sheep that day. The sheep were out there somewhere, I mused, and we had several more days in which to find them. I was confident we would.

We readied early the next morning for the ride back to the fishing camp. It was Halloween Sunday, October 31, but even in midautumn the desert sun quickly warmed the morning air. Our plan was the same as the day before—to glass the sheep trails leading down the canyon walls to the river. Around mid-morning, we had a brief flurry of excitement when Cocese glassed a group of sheep some two miles distant. On closer examination, these were not desert bighorns; they were aoudad (*Ammotragus lervia*). Also known as Barbary sheep, the aoudad is a tough, smart critter.

These impressive-looking animals were introduced to west Texas by returning World War II veterans who had served in North Africa and foreseen the aoudad's potential for game hunting. The game has thrived in the state and is widely hunted on Texas game ranches. Yet

While glassing for sheep along the canyon walls, we became excited when we spotted a distant herd of what we initially thought were bighorns. The critters were actually aoudad sheep, a North African import that thrives in West Texas.

wildlife officials are concerned that the aoudad may be impeding the growth of the Mexican wild sheep herds in West Texas. These non-native Barbary sheep carry a bacterium that can cause a fatal respiratory disease in North American bighorn sheep.

Unfortunately, spotting these aoudads was the only big excitement that day. We stayed in our position above the fishing camp all afternoon, determined to view any bighorn sheep that might come down the sides of the canyon for water. Locals told us the sheep often bed about a third of the way up these canyon walls, but we saw none. With the temperature reaching 105 degrees that afternoon, we called it quits around five o'clock. This was disappointing.

When we returned to base camp, I called a local rancher named Eric Stovall. Barry had told me about this rancher, who owned a large spread just southwest of our lodge. Eric sold landowner permits for desert bighorn on his ranchland and also provided guide service for hunters. He told me over the phone that we probably wouldn't find any sheep where we had been glassing. He advised that we hunt several miles upriver in the direction of Reagan Canyon.

We decided to hunt only one more day. Fortune needed to smile on us soon, or I was looking at a shutout on my first hunt for a desert bighorn.

Reaching the fishing camp around nine, our plans were to hike upriver for a number of miles, so this could turn into a tough day. We took along plenty of water, our trekking poles, and wooden clappers, which we made by strapping two-by-fours together on one end. Slapping these boards together mimics the sound of crashing horns, which is believed to attract desert bighorn rams. Eric had recommended the clappers when I spoke with him by phone. I have heard that some from Texas Park and Wildlife disapproved of this practice, considering it sheep harassment. These "ram callers" were considerable extra weight to carry on our hike, but we hoped they would pay off.

We began walking upstream, hugging the banks as we picked our way along. This was challenging, the riverbanks rocky and steep. In some areas we became "cliffed-out" when the steep sides of the canyon descended directly to the waterline. It took us about three hours to cover the three or four miles upriver—a helluva long jaunt in this canyon terrain.

We came to a dark rock wall that towered over the canyon on the Mexican side of the river. Eric had advised us to situate ourselves near the river at this location and glass the canyon slopes. We ate lunch and began glassing in earnest. The weather that day duplicated the previous two: cloudless, nearly windless, and blisteringly hot in the afternoon. By about three in the afternoon, we gave up on the sheep. Barring a lucky break while hiking back to our ATV, this hunt was a bust.

The demanding return was made even more difficult by the one hundred-plus temperatures that afternoon. It took us a half hour longer going back than coming out. While disappointed with the hunt, we were relieved to throw our gear on the ATV and begin the long ride back to base camp. Swerving along this route reminded me of a kind of dangerous, unregulated amusement ride. At least we had this excitement to distract us from the disappointment of our hunt.

Following a disheartening return to the fishing camp to retrieve my forgotten pack, it was about 8:30 that evening before we plopped our tired bodies down at base camp. My first desert ram hunt was kaput. My hunting permit on the ranch, however, was good until August 31, 2011, so I still had ten months to make good on it.

Before we left for Oklahoma the next morning, I made another call to the rancher Eric Stovall, who earlier had advised us to move our sheep hunt closer to Reagan Canyon. I booked him to guide me on a hunt in mid-January, just a little more than two months away. I would still be on Bear Canyon Ranch, of course, but Eric would take me farther upriver toward Reagan Canyon. Although my first desert ram hunt had been fruitless, I left Texas feeling as if I had a good plan in place for the next.

MY MID-JANUARY HUNTING PLANS went awry when I had to fix both a recurring knee problem and a problem with my Gunwerks LR-1200 rifle. I didn't leave for my second desert ram hunt on Bear Canyon Ranch until mid-July. Taxidermist Mike Chain accompanied me, but his wife, Cocese, stayed in Oklahoma City this time. She had her fill of the harsh country along the Rio Grande. July could be especially difficult, with daytime high temperatures of 110 to 115 degrees.

Just as on the first hunt, we planned to stay in the hunting lodge on the Rhodes family ranch. Our guide, Eric, was to rendezvous with us at the lodge on Friday morning to begin the hunt. Mike and I arrived at the gate to Bear Canyon Ranch about four o'clock on a Thursday afternoon only to find that the water pump for the lodge was broken. We ended up staying with our guide on his Stovall Ranch about ten miles southwest of the hunting lodge.

We were up before dawn for a hearty breakfast of scrambled eggs, bacon and tortillas and soon made our way down a relatively smooth jeep trail on Bear Canyon Ranch as the morning light broke over the desert landscape. Our destination was a Rio Grande overlook called Little Piece of Heaven by locals. The overlook stood several miles southwest and upriver from the fishing camp at the mouth of Bear Canyon, and a couple of miles northeast of where Reagan Canyon opened into the river. On the final day of the previous year's failed hunt, Mike, Cocese and I had cliffed-out along the river just northeast of this Little Piece of Heaven.

The jeep trail to the overlook was much improved over the blasted-out Bear Canyon trail we had bumped along the previous fall. Eric and a professional trapper named Andy led the way in a four-wheeled ATV while Mike and I followed in a six-wheeler. While our two vehicles powered up this high ground, Eric had positioned two helpers along the river to drive any sheep along the steep slopes toward our position.

The trail ascended sharply as we crested a high ridge atop Little Piece of Heaven and overlooking the Rio Grande. Climbing out of the ATV in the whipping wind, I gazed awestruck at the miles of Rio Grande valley stretching below. Most of my previous views of the river had been limited in the confines of canyons. In this area the distant canyon walls on the U.S. side give a wide berth to the winding Rio Grande forming a valley and allowing miles of river view. The broad banks of the river were thick with a heavy growth of trees, shrubs, and other vegetation, creating bright-green swaths beside the water. This riparian growth contrasted sharply with the sun-scorched gray and brown landscape around the valley.

Andy climbed down from the overlook to better view the terraced slopes below us. Eric, Mike and I worked our way around the rim of

From our location in Little Piece of Heaven, the broad Rio Grande valley displayed wide banks with thick swaths of trees, shrubs and other vegetation.

the overlook, intently glassing the sun-scorched slopes. I could see Andy in the distance occasionally arm-signaling to Eric. While I was glassing near a wire fence along the rim about nine o'clock, Andy's excited waving caught my eye. He had spotted a mature desert ram with some ewes after being alerted to their location from our helpers on the river. They saw these bighorns emerge from a cave below us. The sheep were browsing at a distance well below our overlook but within shooting range.

After pinpointing their location with my binoculars, I set up my Gunwerks 7-millimeter rifle and lay prone on a large, limestone slab between two sharp yucca plants. Some four- to five-hundred yards below, my ram and two ewes were feeding near two small mesquite trees. Just beyond the mesquites was a small ridge, a convenient escape route for spooked sheep. The ram's horns made a full curl, definitely a shooter. I looked around impatiently for Mike, who was supposed to be carrying the range finder. Inexplicably, Mike wasn't nearby. I couldn't tell where the hell he was. My heart was pounding, and I concentrated hard to regulate my breathing.

Eric bolted for the ATV to look for the range finder. By the time he returned with the instrument, the ram was getting jittery—and so was I. The animal probably didn't pick up our scent but may have detected the discordant movement above him. Unfamiliar with the range finder, Eric had trouble with it. I stayed glued to my rifle scope, fighting hard to calm myself. Finally, Eric ranged the ram at 450 yards.

With the ram's right shoulder locked in my crosshairs, I slowly squeezed the trigger. Just at the instant I fired, the nervous ram began to turn. He was hit hard but didn't fall. The wounded ram lurched toward concealment over the ridge as I fired again. Andy later said he thought the second shot hit the ram. I fired a third ineffective shot as the ram disappeared.

We had a commanding view from our high ground, so I remained in shooting position on the rock slab. After waiting nearly an hour for the ram to emerge, Andy and one of Eric's helpers began to move along the rugged slopes toward the ram's last position. The trapper believed the wounded sheep to be in a jumble of rocks in a ravine. They picked up a blood trail on some rocks in the ravine and began following it. The dark stains led downward, the usual movement of a wounded sheep. Over his walkie-talkie, Andy reported another group of desert sheep far down on the slopes below. Eric surmised that the wounded ram might be trying to join this group.

Not long before noon, Andy radioed that the blood trail had suddenly played out—but no ram lay at the end. Blood had probably coagulated around the entrance wound and staunched the flow. With early reports from Andy that the ram had been hit in the shoulder and bled profusely, I believed that we would eventually find him dead or mortally wounded. But as midday approached, I grew more and more apprehensive.

We glassed the canyon walls around the ravine where the ram

had seemed to vanish. Andy began a long hike across the river valley toward the ravine. I had to admire his grit as he picked his way through the boulders and up the side of the canyon, in cowboy boots no less. By the time he returned, shadows covered the river valley. We would have to give up the search until the next day.

We arose before daylight the next morning, and Mike and I followed Eric and Andy as we drove to the river. Our plans were to continue searching the area below Little Piece of Heaven. To help bring this hunt to an end, each of us carried a rifle. Our ATVs followed the jeep trail above Reagan Canyon in the early dawn. The early morning temperature was only 68 degrees, and the breeze in the ATV chilled me. A red sky glowed among the low clouds. As daylight brightened, we saw evidence of rainfall from the night before. More rain was desperately needed in this parched region, but I hoped it would hold off until we found my ram.

No such luck. After a morning and early afternoon of futilely searching for my wounded Mexican bighorn, the sky darkened, and a distant sandstorm kicked up. A misty rain soon obscured the canyon walls in the river valley. With the rainstorm washing away any fresh blood from the wounded ram, around five o'clock we decided to make our way back up Reagan Canyon to Eric's house.

A short way up from the river, I felt a little like fate was taunting me when we spotted two rams and a ewe less than two hundred yards from our jeep trail. One ram was nothing short of magnificent. We stopped the ATV, and Mike and I took in this thrilling scene. Uncharacteristically, these wild sheep appeared unperturbed by our barely distant presence.

The mature ram had a chocolate coat, and his horns were slightly over a full curl. He was a beautiful specimen. Taking that ram would have been one of the easiest shots I ever made.

"I wish Eric would tell you to go ahead and shoot that sheep," Mike said half-seriously. "Don't you?"

"Yeah, but he's not gonna do that," I replied wistfully. "No one's gonna make an executive decision like that."

My shooting of the Mexican bighorn the day before was all that was allowed by my permit unless the landowner determined that the ram was alive and well. So I was done on this permit unless Barry

Crumrine said otherwise. If Barry gave me permission to shoot another ram and the previous one turned up dead, it would be hell to pay. Barry and I could end up as cell mates in a Texas penitentiary.

We went out again the next day to search for my ram, but I held little hope that we would find him. We did, however, find a dead mountain lioness. We were in the heart of mountain lion country in Reagan Canyon, Andy explained as we examined the carcass. "There's a number of lions working this part of the canyon," the trapper explained, "and the desert bighorn are number one on the buffet line. They're gonna make a kill about every other night, either deer or sheep."

He said that he checked his traps every two or three days, attempting to be as humane as possible in the taking of the mountain lions. "He's just doing what God intended him to do," he said of these predators.

Contemplating things on the way back to Eric's ranch house, I realized my dire situation with this pricey desert bighorn permit. The permit was only good until the end of August. This was late July, and I already had a hunting trip to Canada lined up for August. If I were to make good on this permit, I needed to do it in the next five weeks and work it around my Canadian trip.

Whether I could hunt again on this permit depended on Barry Crumrine's family. As the seller of this landowner permit, the family would have to determine that my shooting of the ram had not been fatal before allowing me to continue with this same permit. I enlisted Eric and Andy to go to bat for me and explain to Barry how we had found no evidence of a dead ram. They said they would call Barry and do what they could.

Shortly after my return to Oklahoma City, Barry called and told me that he would discuss the situation with his family. The decision to let me continue to hunt on this permit would not be his alone. His extended family would have to reach a consensus on this decision. The permit would expire at the end of August, so I obviously needed to know something soon.

SHORTLY AFTER my mid-August return to Oklahoma City from British Columbia, I called Barry Crumrine. He had discussed the situation with his family, he said, and the consensus was that I had expended the permit. Ouch! That hurt a bit. Still, in all fairness I had taken my bite at the apple when I wounded the ram. I really didn't expect a second bite free of charge, so I could live with it.

And I wanted a desert bighorn even more now. My trip to British Columbia had resulted in a successful Stone thinhorn hunt, so a desert bighorn ram would qualify me for the Grand Slam of North American Wild Sheep. I was certainly willing to pay for another permit to get me closer to this milestone for wild sheep hunters.

Barry added that Texas Parks and Wildlife was at the time completing its annual survey of desert bighorn sheep in the region. He would soon be notified whether Bear Canyon Ranch would receive another permit for the new fiscal hunting year, which ran from September 2011 through August 2012. I readily agreed to purchase another pricey permit to hunt on Bear Canyon Ranch if the landowners were allowed one by state officials.

Early in September, Barry called me with good news. He could sell me a new permit, and the family had agreed to the same relatively low price as before. I immediately called Eric Stovall to see if he would again guide me. The Texas rancher had impressed me with his easygoing manner and his ability to find sheep on my previous desert ram hunt. I told him I wanted to come down as soon as possible to complete my Grand Slam.

Although as affable as usual, he was reluctant to guide me at that time of year. He preferred to hunt the sheep from a boat along the Rio Grande, and the river was low in late summer and early fall. Hunting from a boat this time of year might require a tedious process of unloading and portaging over shallow parts of the channel.

I pressed him, telling him how eager I was to wrap up my Grand Slam. "Okay, we'll try it," he said caving to my lobbying effort.

But Eric had one caveat for taking me out: I would need to come alone. He wanted no one with me that might make a mistake at a critical time in the hunt. I readily agreed to come solo. The only other member of our hunting party would be our packer. For these duties, Eric wanted to take along Andy, the mountain lion trapper who had accompanied us on the previous hunt.

As the hot Oklahoma summer began to ease, I made my final

arrangements for the familiar trip to Bear Canyon Ranch along the "big bend" of the Rio Grande. I packed both my Gunwerks rifle and one of my two Sakos, this one a .338 caliber. The Sako would serve as a backup if I had any problems with the Gunwerks rifle. The LR-1200 had performed flawlessly since the addition of the Night-force scope earlier in the year, and I didn't truly anticipate any issues with it. I was being extra cautious bringing the backup firearm. This would be my third trip to West Texas for a desert ram and my second purchase of a landowner permit. I wanted as little as possible left to chance.

Getting a late start on the last Sunday in September, early Monday morning I drove familiar roads to Alpine to verify the purchase of my new landowner permit with an official at the Texas Parks and Wildlife Department. From there it was on to the small town of Marathon to fill up my gas tank and proceed to Eric Stovall's work-ing ranch. I arrived on the sprawling cattle ranch in late morning.

Eric and Andy were ready to take to the field upon my arrival. The rancher gave a quick overview of our plans, which entailed es-tablishing our base at the fishing camp at the confluence of Bear Canyon and the Rio Grande. Getting there would require the same rocky ride we had taken each day from Barry Crumrine's hunting cabin on my first hunt the previous fall, but a big difference this time would be the use of Eric's shallow-draft boat to patrol the river as we searched for sheep along the canyon walls. The rancher's boat was already docked at the fishing camp.

Early that afternoon, we drove two six-wheel ATVs over the bru-tal jeep trail that paralleled Bear Canyon to its mouth at the river. The stark beauty of this landscape brought back memories of the previous year. That trip had been in mid-autumn, so the tempera-tures were milder, especially early in the day. With fall barely begun on this visit, the early afternoon temperature was already more than 100 degrees. The canyon walls along the river came into view as we descended steeply to the fishing camp.

Our plan for the remainder of the afternoon was to glass for sheep from the boat as we made our way down river to a prime fishing area. Eric planned to lay jug lines for catfish while we hunted sheep. Along the way to the fishing area, we would glass the sides of the canyons and use two-by-four wooden clappers to call the rams. The water level was low, just as Eric feared, so an occasional disembarkation and boat tow might be required.

The river downstream from the fishing camp was new to me, but the towering canyon walls were no less impressive than those upriver. No sign of civilization could be seen along this route. The twists and turns of the river, the occasional boulders rising above the waterline, and the ever-present canyon walls had doubtless changed little since this section of the river was first mapped by U.S. Army engineers in 1853.

Eric's shallow-draft fishing boat was powered by a small, gas-powered motor that could be hand-tilted to raise the propeller in low water. Christened "Jaws" for its distinctive hand-painted shark's teeth on the front of its hull, the versatile craft sat high in the water. The sound of the clappers resounded through the canyons as we trolled down river. I had gone after sheep in airplanes, float planes and ATVs. I had hunted them by horse, by mule and on foot. This, however, was the first time from a boat—which I had to admit was a pretty relaxing way to hunt.

Coming to a rocky, shallow section of the river, Eric steered to the riverbank to drop me off. I stood beside the swiftly moving water with both my rifles and glassed the canyon walls. The real action was in the water, where Eric and Andy were trying to get the boat through the shallow rapids. Eric jumped out and began pushing the boat in the two-foot-deep water. The two river cowboys slowly made their way with the current into deeper water. Eric climbed back into the boat and motored toward me as Andy followed in the waist-deep water. I congratulated the pair on their improvised boating skills as I boarded.

The rancher didn't seem too amused by all this drama. I remembered that he had tried to postpone this hunt until the river was higher. When we had first boarded the boat, he showed me a patched area in the bottom of the boat that resulted from an accident involving a river rock. The patch consisted of an epoxy-like substance that sealed the hole in the hull. Eric hoped to avoid more repairs like that.

With all Eric's jug lines deployed by five o'clock, we motored back upriver leaving a trail of bobbing plastic containers. The occasional slap of our clappers echoed through the canyons. "Ease up, ease up," Andy exclaimed. He pointed toward a low ridge at the bottom of a steep canyon wall. I followed his line and spotted a handsome desert bighorn ram about two hundred yards off and moving parallel with the river. He quickly vanished into a low spot on the other side of the ridge. We slowed the boat to a crawl and kept our eyes glued on the ridge. Andy let out a long, slow whistle. I couldn't tell if this was in recognition of the ram's size or an attempt to lure him back in the open.

"There he is, there he is," I cried out as the ram came back into view. He walked nonchalantly along the side of the ridge. He saw and heard us, but, oddly, didn't seem overly concerned. I was ready to get to the riverbank and set up for the shot.

"He's brooming, but he's too young," Eric said. "Check him out with your glasses."

I heard this disappointing news from my guide but wasn't convinced this ram was too young to shoot. "He's in good shape," I countered as I glassed him.

"He's got some mass," Andy confirmed.

"He could get shot over that mass," Eric added. "Yeah, he's not running with no ewes." This was rutting season, and a mature ram would probably be found near ewes.

The ram stopped and turned directly toward us. He stared and we stared back.

"Damn," I said. "I wish you guys would let me shoot him." He looked too good to pass up, but Eric kept the boat in the middle of the channel. I fought the urge to leap from the boat and wade to shore with my rifle.

Giving in to my guide, I slapped the clappers. This was done more to see the ram's reaction than anything. Perhaps I subconsciously wanted to drive him from my sight and end my frustration. At the sound of the clappers the young ram scampered for higher ground. His gait was measured, not panicked. We watched the ram as he made his way to the crest of the ridge. Eric and Andy joked about how embarrassed they would be to let me shoot a sheep that young.

"Oh, my gosh," I said wistfully as the ram vanished over the ridgeline. No question I would have taken the shot if they had not insisted that the ram was an adolescent. As we resumed our boat ride up the river, Andy consoled me with a reminder that the clappers seemed to have initially drawn the young ram out. They might later work just as well with a mature ram. With the late afternoon sunlight casting long shadows in the canyon, we continued back upriver to the fishing camp.

Our shelter at the fishing camp consisted of an uninhabitable trailer connected to a large carport. The untenable trailer had filled up over the years with the detritus of past hunts and fishing expeditions. Even venturing into the trailer for a quick look required courage. Who knew what menacing desert creatures lurked among the boxes and junk. Although only a roof without walls, the airy carport appeared free of desert crawlers and offered shelter in the unlikely event of rain. Several small, metal bed frames were scattered across the deteriorating concrete floor of the carport. Just outside the trailer, an abandoned refrigerator gaped open. We brought enough food, water and beer for several days, which we kept cool in large ice chests. The small mattresses we brought snugly fit the metal bed frames, and the cool night air made for good sleeping.

The Rio Grande moved along placidly just below our campsite,

The carport at the fishing camp provided shelter in the event of rain, one of the few amenities of our otherwise spartan living quarters along the river.

much as it had for millennia. Viewing the water from a distance, it appeared brown and muddy. But on closer examination, the river's dingy look was only a reflection of the sand that swirled in its flow. Cupping a handful of the river, the sand settled on my palm and the water cleared. That evening we stripped down and waded into the current to wash the sweat and grime from our afternoon's efforts. Standing in the water and gazing at the high canyon walls on the Mexican side of the river, I thought of the countless Native Americans, vaqueros, soldiers, bandits, cowboys and hunters who also had cooled and cleansed in this section of the storied Rio Grande over the last few centuries.

Before dinner, we snacked on what the locals call "poppers"— grilled Jalapeno peppers stuffed with cheese and secret ingredients. Eric and Andy were aficionados of this treat, which went well with the cold beer from the coolers. Our main course was beefsteak, cooked on our propane grill. Our appetites sated, we languished in the cool evening air, listening to the soft slapping of the river on its long journey to the Gulf of Mexico.

I lit up a cigar and luxuriated in my exotic surroundings, gazing upriver at the black canyon walls where the river below occasionally glistened in the moonlight. The stars sparkled brilliantly in the dry, unpolluted atmosphere. How little these desert lands had changed over the last century, and how quiet and empty they seemed that evening.

Yet real drama filled these borderlands a hundred years earlier when Mexican outlaw bands frequently raided Texas settlements. The wily Mexican political bandit Francisco "Pancho" Villa had stirred things up early in 1916 when his outlaw-revolutionaries raided across the border into Columbus, New Mexico, and killed seventeen Americans. Led by Brigadier General John "Blackjack" Pershing, a punitive force of nearly five thousand American soldiers chased Villa and his band across northern Mexico and in the vicinity of the future Big Bend National Park.

Our peaceful campsite seemed far removed from these events as I finished off my cigar that late September evening. It was hard to imagine that thousands of U.S. troops had once massed in this area and crossed the Rio Grande into Mexico. It was much easier that quiet evening to envision occasional Mexican emigrants furtively crossing the river in search of economic opportunities. Although the fishing camp had probably seen plenty of use by these Mexican émigrés over the years, we saw none during our stay.

Lying in bed before sleep overtook me, I couldn't stop thinking about that good-looking ram that Eric had prevented me from shooting that afternoon. Both Eric and Andy had viewed that ram far differently than I had. They even used the term "baby" to describe it. The way I saw it, that ram was somewhere from seven to nine years old, certainly no "baby" and actually prime age for shooting. Even if that sheep were younger than he appeared, I still could have taken a good set of horns and would now be drifting off to sleep with my Grand Slam secured.

This was my third trip to this area over the previous eleven months. Taking a desert ram had proved more elusive than my Dall, Rocky Mountain and Stone prizes. Going back to Oklahoma City again without having taken a desert bighorn would make for a long, miserable ride home. I normally slept well in the outdoors on my hunts; that night I didn't. My mind's eye kept seeing that ram from earlier in the afternoon—the ram that I didn't shoot.

Arising about dawn the next morning, we ate a leisurely breakfast of scrambled eggs and bacon before loading our boat. The towering golden-brown walls on the Mexican side of the river opposite our fishing camp appeared more impressive in the morning sunlight. Both the beauty and the ruggedness of the area continued to impress me. Canyon walls dominated our fishing camp in every direction. The areas below these walls were covered in ocotillo and cholla cactus, and other kinds of potentially painful flora.

Loaded with guns and gear, we cruised down river to check the trotlines we had deployed the day before. The low water forced me to disembark several times while Andy and Eric pushed and pulled the boat. Two of the plastic jugs had mysteriously vanished. Several others provided a nice haul of catfish. We made our way back upriver to unload the catch at the fishing camp.

We left the fishing camp mid-morning on our way upriver toward the Little Piece of Heaven overlook where I had wounded the ram two months earlier. Our route paralleled the hike from the fishing camp that I had taken the year before with Mike and Cocese. Trolling in the boat was easier than that hot slog along the riverbank we had endured, with its occasional rocky detours when the trail cliffed-out. This third hunt covered familiar ground—all too familiar to me. Would I ever get out of these sunbaked canyons with a desert ram to my credit?

As we continued upriver, the views of the steep canyon walls grew even more enchanting. This section of the Rio Grande, beginning just past the east border of Big Bend National Park, has the designation of National Wild and Scenic River—special rivers or sections of rivers set aside by Congress for preservation in their free-flowing state. The river meanders generally eastward for more than eighty miles through the Lower Canyons of the Rio Grande. We were boating only a few miles of these pristine canyons, but more than a thousand daring souls float the entire Wild and Scenic River section of the Rio Grande each year. Their river adventure in this remote borderland ends at the "Dryden takeout," some fifty miles east and down river from our fishing camp.

A number of feral cattle grazed along the riverbank on the U.S. side as we made our way farther upriver. This wild livestock can be hunted by anyone, and locals occasionally round up some of these cattle for a barbecue. These bovine foragers have ruined delicate areas of riverbank by stripping away vegetation that maintains the fragile soil. This has turned some stretches of the riverbank into unsightly, sandy wastelands.

"Well, do you want to get your bull hunt done, Leonard," Eric joked as we motored past a tough-looking feral bull.

"We could," I said playing along. "Want me to shoot him?"

"We need to have Andy go up there and hotshot him, so he'd be a more challenging shot from the boat," Eric bantered.

I occasionally sounded the clappers as we continued our slow boat ride upriver. Several miles down river from Reagan Canyon, I saw the dark, towering rock wall on the Mexican side of the river, which was opposite the position where Mike, Cocese and I glassed for several hours the previous fall. This was the area that Eric had advised our small party to hike to following two sheepless days of glassing near the fishing camp. A little before noon my eyes fixed on the exact rocky perch from where we had patiently and futilely glassed the surrounding canyon walls. Here I was on my third hunt along this river, right back to where we had hoped to take a desert ram on the first hunt a year earlier.

As I gazed at those familiar rocks along the riverbank, Andy stiffened and fixed his gaze on the lower cliffs above the U.S. side of the river. "Look up there! Look up there!" the trapper exhorted pointing toward the towering walls.

I strained my eyes in the direction he pointed but saw only steep, rocky cliff with the usual assortment of uninviting cactus and bushes. "There's the big one," Andy said, eyes still fixed. By that time Eric was steering the boat toward a clump of mesquite trees on the relatively flat riverbank on the Mexican side of the river.

Scouring the steep, rocky cliff, I began to see bighorn sheep several hundred yards up the side. The ewes and rams blended in almost perfectly in the background of dusty brown cliffside. My eyes seized on the probable leader of this group—a mature ram displaying an impressive set of horns on a large, muscular frame. He was bedded and partially obscured by some large rocks. Another mature male mingled with the ewes but had not the body nor horns of the ram that had grabbed my attention. I felt a surge of adrenaline as my heart began to pound. This was it!

As the boat lodged against the sandy shoreline, I scrambled up the riverbank shaking like a leaf. Eric and I hurried into the mesquite grove, and I hastily set up my Bog-Pod shooting rest. I adjusted the legs of this tripod so that I could shoot upward at close to a forty-five-degree angle while seated on the sandy riverbank. I quickly had the big ram in my crosshairs. Eric ranged the sheep at two hundred yards.

"When that ram stands up, you need to shoot him," my guide stated unequivocally.

Those were my sentiments exactly. I would have to wait until the ram showed more because the large rocks partially shielded him from view. By this time the sheep were looking directly at us. My heart thudded as I sat in the shade of the mesquites waiting for the ram to stand.

Frozen like statues, the three of us stared upward at the distant ram across the river. No words passed between us. I forced deep, steady breaths. My heart pounded harder as the ram began a slow rise to his feet. Standing, he was still partly shielded by a large rock. Then he began a slow move to an opening between the boulders. He was as good a specimen of a desert bighorn as I could have hoped for. As soon as he presented himself in full view, I locked the cross-hairs on his front shoulder.

As soon as I fired, the ram spun and dropped where he stood. Eric and Andy yelled and hooted in celebration. I think they shared my relief. The other sheep reacted in a confused manner, as is usually the case with the death of their leader. Even with all of our whooping and high-fiving, these sheep didn't spook.

"Well, buddy, you own this herd now," Eric said to me as we watched the sheep.

"Man, oh, man..." I responded, almost at a loss for words and

My third hunt in West Texas, an effort straddling two calendar years, finally resulted in my first desert bighorn prize. This also brought on a case of desert sheep fever. To my right is Texas rancher and my guide, Eric Stovall.

in disbelief that I had taken this wonderful specimen of a ram. Although relatively short at two hundred yards, this shot had been international, fired from the Mexican side of the river to drop a ram on U.S. soil. A noteworthy achievement, and completely legal.

As the formerly dominant ram lay dead nearby, the other male in the group began courting and sniffing one of the ewes. "He's working the same ewe that the big boy was working," Eric said. "He's just inherited a herd."

"It was his lucky day and mine, too," I quipped.

Andy complimented Eric on his scouting of these sheep. Several days earlier, Eric had boated by these cliffs and spotted this group and the big ram. Eric noted that the sheep had not moved more than a quarter mile from where he had first seen them.

With the sheep showing few signs of leaving, we were content to watch this scene while sitting on the riverbank. At that moment, just taking a desert ram seemed about as satisfying to me as having qualified for Grand Slam designation. Of the four required sheep, this one had been the most difficult to bag.

This was also my first ram taken with the full blessing of one of my guides. I shot my Dall, Rocky Mountain and Stone sheep with my guides either startled by my shot or advising me not to shoot. Finally, on the last of my four Grand Slam rams, my guide and I were completely in sync at the moment of truth, and this desert ram looked to be close to trophy class. In the end everything had come together almost perfectly in the coup de grâce for my Grand Slam.

Sitting comfortably in the shade of the mesquites, we were content to wait until the sheep eased off on their own before proceeding to inspect my ram. As we watched the distant scene, buzzards soon began to circle high above the kill site. Almost on cue, the young ram and ewes began to amble up the side of the cliff. A chapter ended and a new chapter began in the cycle of life in that harsh land along the Rio Grande.

"Well, they've figured out that big daddy's not coming with 'em," Eric said as he looked through his binoculars. "They're probably starting to smell the blood."

"Now comes the job of hiking up there," Andy said. "I know it doesn't look very far, but I'm sure we'll all have thoroughly enjoyed it by the time we get off there with him."

"It's a hundred ninety-nine yards if we could fly," Eric said, "but it's gonna feel like a mile."

We boarded our boat to cross the river and claim my trophy ram. The full weight of the midday sun bore down and the temperature registered 110 degrees. After crossing the river, I put on leather gloves to protect against the hot rocks we climbed as we made our way up the steep cliff side. The scramble to my ram took nearly a half hour. We stopped several times along the way, panting in the withering heat.

As we cleared an outcropping of boulders, the dead ram came into full view. He looked almost restful as he lay curled among the rocks on the limestone-flecked soil. Approaching the downed ram, I saw an unusual amount of blood on the rocks and resurrection plants behind him. On closer examination I saw that the bullet had passed completely through. I straddled the ram and pulled on his horns to lift his head. His upper body rippled with muscle and mass.

"Oh, he's gonna go one seventy easy," Andy exclaimed. (The final Boone and Crockett score for this ram was actually 159.)

I turned the ram's head in several directions to view the sizable set of horns, which finished their curl at eye level. "I can't believe this," I gushed. "Oh, my gosh."

After taking a series of pictures, the tedious task of skinning and butchering the ram began. I left this job largely in the hands of Eric and Andy, with their work made more difficult by the scorching afternoon sun. As they carefully skinned the ram, I got a better idea of the years on this Rio Grande royalty. The twelve-year-old hide was thick and tough. Andy struggled to cut through the hard cartilage at the base of the ram's horns.

After the skinning was completed, I posed for more pictures with the head and horns. "Well, you just completed your big four Grand Slam, Leonard," Eric pronounced as I held up the trophy for another photo.

"And what a way to complete it with this guy," Andy added pointing to the horns.

"I still can't believe it," I said. "This is a lifetime hunting dream. I'm not kidding you."

North American Desert Sheep Hunting

Andy led the way down the steep cliff toward the river, which appeared green and placid far below. Going down wasn't much easier than our earlier climb up, but this mattered little to me. My rifle and pack felt light as a feather. I had my desert bighorn ram—and would soon have my official Grand Slam designation. Eight years earlier I had started along this adventurous journey in the Chugach Mountains where I had initially failed to take a Dall thinhorn. From there I had hunted the slopes of the Alaska Range, and later the high ridgelines of the Wapiti Ridge in Wyoming. After two frustrating hunts along the Rio Grande, the Grand Slam adventure was coming to an end along these canyons of west Texas borderland. What a thrilling ride it had been.

We made our way back down the river to our fishing camp in the afternoon swelter. With my desert ram's head and horns now safely packed away, I could better appreciate this river scenery. The boat ride through some of the shallow areas and rapids was made easier by our going with the current, rather than against it as we had earlier. I again marveled at how this mighty Rio Grande, which starts its journey in the majestic Rocky Mountains of Colorado, is almost unbelievably shallow in some parts of these canyonlands, less than a foot deep in some spans. I carefully guarded my trophy through some of these rough, shallow stretches of river, with short stints pulling the boat.

As we motored into the fishing camp at the end of our boat ride, I was taken aback to see a startlingly attractive woman walking down to the river. Eric's friend, Jennifer, had come out to greet us on our triumphant return. She congratulated me on my hunting success, a pleasant surprise at the end of the hunt.

That evening at Eric's ranch house we feasted on the catfish taken on the trotlines. We decided to forego the tough, sinewy meat of the grizzled old ram. He would make a great mount, but his years disqualified him for good dining fare. Lounging about after dinner, I lit up a cigar. Eric, Andy and I had some things to discuss. Chief topic of our conversation was the aoudad hunt on tap for the next day. With my desert ram and Grand Slam secured, I was looking forward to a quick hunt for one of these exotic sheep transplants from North Africa.

We boated back to the fishing camp along the Rio Grande with my prized desert ram aboard. We later feasted on a catfish dinner as my aged ram's meat was too tough for a good meal. From left, Eric, Andy and me.

THE AOUDAD HUNT proved unproductive, but I wasn't too disappointed. I had my first desert bighorn ram and my Grand Slam of North American Wild Sheep. Over those three hunts in the Big Bend region, I had also learned some valuable lessons about hunting desert sheep, an outdoor recreation that would rapidly become a passion for me. Besides learning to more carefully evaluate a ram before pulling the trigger, I came to appreciate the importance of a good guide who knows where and how to find a good ram. Eric Stovall had obviously been one of those knowledgeable locals, but I had wasted my first hunt for a desert bighorn before I found him. I later learned that one of the wildlife officials in Alpine could also have guided me.

With my taking of the Mexican bighorn ram, I qualified for my Grand Slam, but I was on my way to another designation just as fun and possibly even more challenging—a personal "grand slam" of desert bighorn sheep. One down, three to go. I could hardly wait for the next desert adventure.

CHAPTER 3

A *Mexicana* Hunt in Sonora

(2014)

My quest for a Sonoran Desert bighorn ram started at the January 2014 Dallas Safari Club Convention when an outfitter's booth caught my attention. Or perhaps I should say the striking photos of Sonoran Desert bighorn rams at this booth caught my attention.

The photos were displayed by an attendant named Sergio, who was manning the booth for outfitting service Sonora Dark Horn Adventures. The service operates out of Tucson, Arizona, but guides in the state of Sonora in northwest Mexico. Yes, I already had a *mexicana* subspecies from the hunt in 2011 near Big Bend National Park in Texas, which had completed my first Grand Slam of North American wild sheep. But the desert bighorns Sergio showed were more impressive than my prize. And it suddenly dawned on me that if I took a Stone sheep in August that year, a hunt already booked, then I could wrap up my second wild sheep Grand Slam with a Sonoran Desert bighorn. As an added bonus, I could hunt in an exotic region completely new to me.

Very quickly I decided to secure a hunt with Sonora Dark Horn Adventures while at the Dallas convention. Yet Sergio informed me that the outfitter was booked for 2014. Would I like to book a hunt for 2015? Somewhat deflated, I told him I would consider it. I took the pricing and information, and told Sergio I would get back to him.

A month or so later, I approached Sergio again at his booth at the Safari Club International Convention in Las Vegas. My schedule was clear for a December desert ram hunt. Now if I could just get Sonora Dark Horn to squeeze me into their already crowded schedule for 2014. Sergio remembered me when I greeted him and listened sympathetically to my pleas for a December hunt that could complete my second wild sheep slam. (I was optimistically assuming a successful Stone ram hunt in August, which was not at all a foregone conclusion.)

Sergio put a big smile on my face when he finally agreed to book my hunt for December. I left Las Vegas with two sheep hunts scheduled for later that year, both in wild and scenic places. What a great year of hunting lay ahead for 2014!

A little more than two months after my enjoyable—and successful—August multi-species hunt in British Columbia, I flew from Oklahoma City to Dallas on the morning of December 2, and from there to Tucson to meet my ride to the state of Sonora in northwest Mexico. I was in "position A" for another Grand Slam of wild sheep after having taken a Stone ram in British Columbia.

I had been told to prepare to hike ten miles a day in mountainous terrain on this desert bighorn hunt in Mexico. My training earlier that year for the British Columbia hunt and subsequent workouts that fall had me feeling pretty fit as the plane touched down in Tucson. Fabin, a Sonora Dark Horn representative, picked me up at the airport. He served as a driver, packer and good public relations man for the outfitting service. We had a lively conversation on our nearly seven-hour drive to the outfitter's ranch house in Sonora.

Driving straight south from Tucson, we came to the border town of Nogales in about an hour. We had no trouble getting through customs, especially since I had decided not to bring my rifle into Mexico. The paperwork for this had appeared daunting, plus I mistakenly believed that I would have to pay $600 for a firearms permit. My outfitter had assured me that he would provide me with a rifle, but I would later regret failing to bring my own.

From Nogales, we proceeded south on a good highway, but the Mexican towns we passed were a bit rundown. We were skirting the eastern side of the Sonoran Desert, so I didn't really expect resort

Dominated by the distinctive saguaro cactus, the Sonoran Desert landscape in northwestern Mexico has a rugged beauty all its own—both enchanting and intimidating.

communities. About 100 miles south of the border we came to the town of Santa Ana, and from here the road got rough. No more paved highway as we made our way some 150 miles or more southwesterly.

We crossed the center plains of the state of Sonora and through the heart of the Sonoran Desert. The terrain in this western part of the state is largely arid and semi-arid, with some moisture from the Pacific Ocean. While most of the rainfall is on the eastern side of Sonora, much of the runoff finds it way to the western coastal plains on its way to the Gulf of California, also called the Sea of Cortez. We would be hunting mostly in the coastal region north and east of Tiburon Island, the large island in the gulf just off the coast of western Sonora. The ranch house where I would stay at night was only fifteen miles or so from the gulf waters.

Spiked with the distinctive, columnar saguaro cactus unique to the Sonoran Desert, the rugged landscape of the region is both intimidating and enchanting. Ninety percent of the state of Sonora has desert or arid conditions. High temperatures in summer approach

100 degrees but the dry air cools off rapidly at night. The eastern side of the state rises with the high mountains of the Sierra Madre Occidental range, but the western parts are mostly rocky, steep hills and ridges that rise abruptly from the surrounding semi-desert terrain. Large ranches in this western region provide much of the hunting domain for Sonora Dark Horn Adventures.

Despite this rocky, harsh environment, a wide variety of animal and plant species have adapted. Although the higher areas are noted for desert bighorn rams, dozens of other mammals thrive, including mule deer and Coues deer. A wide variety of bird species also make a living off the exotic plants in the region. The saguaro cactus may rule over this harsh landscape, but other varieties of cactus are visible in abundance, including the organ pipe, barrel, cholla, beavertail, prickly pear, and hedgehog.

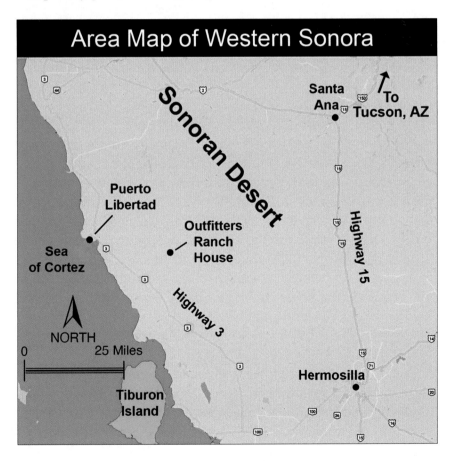

My outfitter's main ranch house was a modern oasis surrounded by the rugged hills of the Sonoran Desert. Except for a scarcity of hot water, the accommodations were comfortable and well maintained.

We arrived at my outfitter's main ranch house about eight that evening. Sergio was there to greet me. The Spanish-style ranch house had the classic cream-colored stucco walls and red-clay tile roof. It was just as elegant on the inside, with modern, stylish furnishings. Although the sun had set before our arrival, I could see low, rugged hills near one side of the house. These mounds of rock in the area don't attain a great height, but I would soon learn that they are steep and inhospitable.

I stowed my gear in my private bedroom, which had the luxury of a private bathroom. My accommodations were largely on par with a first-rate hotel, except for a shortage of hot water. Getting a hot shower would become challenging during my stay.

That evening I met outfitter Raul Cordova, one of the principal owners of Sonora Dark Horn Adventures, and my guide for this adventure, Rick Ortega, who ranches near Las Cruces, New Mexico. Also at the ranch house was Ray Bunney, one of the hosts of the series "Choose Your Weapon" on My Outdoor TV. Learning that I had not brought my own rifle, Ray generously offered to let me shoot with his HS Precision rifle, but I declined. My Outdoor TV was just one of several groups that would be shooting film on deer hunting in the area.

Three other hunters at the hacienda had come to hunt mule deer and Coues deer. The two from Montana would be having their hunt videotaped for a broadcast of some kind. I also planned to hunt deer on this outing, but only after I had achieved my primary goal—one of the impressive desert bighorns that frequent this area.

I was up by four-thirty the next morning, eager to get the day started. My guide Rick would be taking me to the shooting range to get me comfortable with one of the outfitter's rifles. Killing time outside the ranch house before we left, I was impressed by the large solar panels on the grounds. All the electrical power at the ranch house was supplied by the sun.

At the practice range I set up to try the .300-caliber Winchester magnum loaned to me. I fired at the center ring of a target at 100 yards distant. I missed the entire board—several times. We returned to the ranch house to retrieve three more rifles to try out. I had plenty of trouble with the compensators and couldn't get the scope reticles focused for my eye. I made up my mind right then and there to always bring my own rifle to these kinds of hunts, regardless of the hassle and fees.

Outfitter Raul came to my rescue, loaning me his personal rifle, a 6.5-millimeter Gunwerks system with a 140-grain bullet. I had grown comfortable with my own Gunwerks rifle, and I was dead on with this loaner. This was a real relief, but it had taken the entire morning to settle on this firearm. I was impressed with and grateful for the patience my guide and outfitter had shown getting me accustomed to the loaner.

Rick, our wrangler Rubin, and I drove out in Rick's pickup to glass for sheep, bumping along dirt roads in the midday sun. The landscape embodied that exotic desert beauty of cactus, rock-covered hills and bright sunlight. The stately saguaro jutted from the desert floor in every direction. Many of these desert monarchs were a hundred years old or more, my guide told me. The saguaro does not form its distinctive branches (arm-like projections) until reaching age forty or older.

An array of other desert vegetation grew among the saguaro. Much of this unusual-looking growth looked as if it could inflict pain on a hapless hiker. It again reminded me of that old adage about desert flora and fauna: If it don't bite you, it'll stick you. Yet it was all strangely beautiful and serene in the bright sunlight.

My outfitter owned 36,000 acres of this ranchland and leased another 36,000. Although technically desert lands, this area is blessed with the temperature-moderating winds and moisture of the Gulf of California, only a little more than a dozen miles to the west. Some parts of this desert give way to grassy rangeland, similar to parts of the semi-arid Texas Panhandle—if those Texas plains were studded with fifteen-foot-high saguaro cactus.

We quickly began seeing ewes and rams along the rocky hillsides. After checking out one unimpressive ram, we ate lunch at a nearby ranch house. Driving to a nearby area, we glassed a bachelor group of four rams. These rams were just beyond juveniles, but I was

An exotic array of desert vegetation grew among the stately saguaro. Most of this growth could quickly inflict pain on an observer who drew too close.

59

encouraged to see them. Driving to another area, we glassed a small group of ewes and rams, and one of these had potential. I studied him closely with the spotting scope.

The *Ovis canadensis mexicana* has adapted to the dry conditions and sometimes searing temperatures in the mountains and foothills of the arid and semi-arid state of Sonora. Their diet consists largely of desert vegetation. During the cooler, wetter months of winter, they can go for months without drinking water, getting most of their necessary hydration from dew and plants. Even during the hot summers, they can go for long periods without drinking.

Their thick horns can grow to a length of more than forty inches. These strong horns serve mainly as weapons to establish dominance and breeding rights. In the cactus-covered desert areas, this rack substitutes as a tool for breaking open juicy cactus for consumption. The fierce combat undergone by mature rams is evidenced in their scarred and chipped horns. Their horns are usually broken on their tips (broomed) both from fighting and scraping against rocks.

The ram that I scrutinized that afternoon was not a combat veteran. His horns still had the unbroomed "lamb tips" of a young male. And they didn't have the mass and full curl associated with a mature male bighorn. He would probably get there in a few years, but I didn't think he qualified as a shooter.

Rick said he knew of another ram that I would like better, but he was usually found in a rugged area that would require considerable physical effort, lots of hiking and climbing in rough terrain. We didn't have enough daylight to pursue the ram that day. This big ram would be our first pursuit the next morning, my guide said.

By late that afternoon the temperature approached ninety degrees, and I soon stripped down to a T-shirt. Even this far south I had expected cooler temperatures in December. I had already experienced a snow storm three months earlier in British Columbia.

On our way back to the ranch house, Rick stopped by an old, abandoned hacienda to check on a baby goat put out to lure in a troublesome mountain lion. These felines are the primary predator of local sheep and deer. Rick said that he had just recently came upon a Coues deer that had been killed by one of these big desert cats.

Even before viewing the penned-up goat, I could hear it. Its plaintive bleat sounded more like a crying child than an animal. The goat was inside a metal cage to protect it, but its wavering cry emphasized its distress. The desperate pleas from this goat sounded like a good way to attract a big cat—and a good way to give someone chills.

Rubin fed and watered the goat as I checked out the old ranch house. The stucco structure appeared solid, though Rick said the old homestead was well over a hundred years old. It probably had seen good times, but it looked empty and forlorn as I explored it. Even when it had been occupied, the house would have been pretty isolated in this lonely, semi-arid setting.

The rest of the hunters and guides had returned to the ranch house before we came in late that afternoon. As I rested nearby, Rick and Rubin had a long, intense conversation in Spanish. They spoke rapidly, so I caught nothing of their conversation. I supposed they were discussing plans for the next day's sheep hunt.

The steak dinner that evening was excellent, as were all the meals during my stay. A local version of Jalapeno poppers was part of the dining fare. This delightful grilled appetizer was made from Jalapeno peppers wrapped with bacon and shrimp. With the gulf waters just a short drive away, seafood was plentiful in the area.

Just before four in the morning, I awoke to the sound of rain. Packing for this desert hunt, I had not thought to bring rain gear. My outfitter in British Columbia had introduced me to a new brand of hunting apparel in Canada, so I put this lightweight clothing on. It was supposed to have much of the qualities of rain gear, and it would be much cooler than what I had worn the day before.

After breakfast, Rick, Rubin and I took off in the pickup. The rain had stopped at daybreak, but it was still overcast with the temperature in the mid-50s. The desert landscape looked somewhat lush and green as we drove to the low mountains where the big ram had been seen. Rick said the year had been wetter than usual, and the rain during the night had freshened up the vegetation.

We parked the truck and began hiking in the rocky hillocks. I walked between Rick and Rubin, and these outdoorsmen set a blistering pace. Much of this route was uphill. I made good use of my trekking poles, which are always a big help to me on uneven ground.

Rick had said we had a lot of terrain to cover.

After we hiked a while, Rubin said something in Spanish to my guide, who looked at me and grinned. "Rubin said you are *fuerte*, strong hiker," my guide said to me.

That made me feel good. My training was paying off.

We soon made a gradual ascent of a long ridge and began looking for Rick's big ram. With the weather still cool and overcast, it was pleasant glassing from this high ground. The landscape didn't look too desert-like with the recent rain and the somewhat foggy conditions. As comfortable as it was glassing from the ridge, we needed to move on. We weren't seeing sheep.

We trekked to another area and were soon were doing more climbing than hiking. We were often on all fours churning up some of the steeper areas. This reminded me of some of those brutal mountainsides in the Cassiar Mountains of British Columbia. I hadn't really thought that sheep hunting in the Sonoran desert would be so uphill. This was hard going.

We literally crawled to the top of a steep knob and began glassing for Rick's big ram. The three of us were sweating profusely from our exertions, but my new hunting apparel was performing well. It had protected me from the thorns and stickers as we bushwhacked up the knob, and it was efficiently wicking away perspiration. This rapid drying would keep me from getting chilled.

The surrounding terrain was exceptionally rugged—rocks, ridges, vertical bluffs and cactus in all directions. The flat top of the knob was covered in varieties of desert cactus. In addition to the classic saguaro and the squat barrel cactus, numerous organ pipe cactus surrounded our position. Named for their multiple limbs jutting up from the base, these organ pipe cacti looked like plants from another planet—or perhaps a mutant variety of saguaro. The barrel cactus resembled gigantic cucumbers with a thick layer of protective thorns.

My guide pointed out a particularly hazardous plant that seemed to be peculiar to the higher areas of this region. The Spanish word he used for this growth sounded like *yerva-flecha*. (I never could pronounce it to Rick's satisfaction.) If touched by a human, this dangerous plant transmitted a toxin that could induce diarrhea. Yikes!

Our hiking and glassing included navigating rocky, up-and-down terrain covered by the usual variety of intimidating vegetation. Still, the views across the surrounding landscape were enchanting.

Besides worries about being bitten or stuck by the flora and fauna, visitors to the Sonoran Desert have this additional concern.

We glassed for about a half hour. The view was slightly obscured by the fog and haze, a carryover from the rain during the night. No sheep came into view, so it was time to relocate. Our plan was to cross over a large, distant ridge, giving us a new view of the surrounding landscape.

We began the long trek to the other side of the ridge—a hike not near as strenuous as our earlier crawl up the knob. By late morning the sun was out, and our views of the area improved. These hills weren't high in elevation, but their steepness and rocks generally made for rough going. We stopped to glass the distant slopes as we made our way over the ridge.

Once over the ridge, we were high enough to see the rocky hillside where we had sized up the ram the day before. We set up on a small knob and began to glass. The almost-mature bighorn was still in the same area and with what looked to be the same small group of rams and ewes. Rick's big ram, however, was still not in sight. We thought he might still be out there somewhere, perhaps bedded down after a big breakfast.

The strategy was to keep glassing from these high places while staying below the skyline, as human silhouettes can spook the sheep even at a great distance. Using the spotting scopes, the rams could be assessed. Once settling on a prized ram, then it would be a matter of planning the stalk to make the kill. The procedure is fairly simple; the hard part is the hiking and climbing to get into these high places to spot the rams. That's why it's so important for a sheep hunter to train beforehand. If he can't get to the high, remote places, he probably won't find the sheep.

Still not seeing Rick's prize ram, we began the move to another area. This entailed a rigorous jaunt down and then back up to the top of another ridge. The final ascent to this ridge was similar to the brutal climb from earlier in the day, down on all fours and scrambling almost vertically up an escarpment just below the top of the ridge. We planned to follow this long ridgeline, glassing the distant hillsides along the way.

Finally, we spotted a distant group of sheep on the slopes of an impressive promontory that I dubbed the "Rock of Gibraltar." One side of this immense projection went from really steep to near vertical close to the top. The other side sloped off gently into the surrounding terrain. Even from several miles distant, we could see a few rams in this group with our spotting scopes.

Before pursuing this new group, we decided to make one last foray into another area to find Rick's big ram. If we didn't find him, we would redirect our efforts toward the rams near that Gibraltar-like projection in the distance.

We trudged eastward for a new view that might reveal the ram that Rick was so high on. Arriving in this lower area, Rick and Rubin diligently scoured the surrounding slopes through the spotting scopes. Still no big ram. I had about given up on finding Rick's bighorn. The dazzling scenery in the afternoon sun was distracting. The undulating rocky hills went on for miles in every direction, with occasional patches of desert floor in between. This wild Sonoran scenery was still new and enchanting to me.

Top: Setting up the spotting scopes in the cool morning air gave us an eagle's view of the surrounding terrain. This landscape was unlike anything I had experienced in the States. Bottom: The only sheep in the area were near the distant Gibraltar-like knob, which was miles in the distance and would entail a difficult trek across challenging ridges and slopes.

65

North American Desert Sheep Hunting

Rick finally gave up on finding his elusive trophy bighorn, and we began the three-mile trek back toward the rams by my Gibraltar. The miles were adding up this day. I remembered being told that I might have to hike as much as ten miles a day on this adventure, so I had known what to expect. As we got nearer to this group of rams, we found a good place to set up the spotting scopes. It wasn't long before my guide had picked out a shooter from this group. He was bedded down, so we should have some time for our approach.

We hatched a quick plan. Hiking to the base of a ridge adjacent to the ram, we would ascend the ridge out of view of our quarry, and then stalk within rifle range. At the time it didn't look like too difficult a trek, just a long walk.

We hiked along the ridgeline to the overlook above the rams. Getting into position required some steep climbing, but Rick soon had the sheep in his spotting scope. Several of these rams qualified as shooters, but my guide selected the biggest of the group. Guessing

As difficult as it was to ascend the rocky ridges above the desert floor, scrambling up to those distant high places gave us a commanding view of the areas inhabited by sheep.

From our rocky perch overlooking a group of rams, we ranged the biggest at 850 yards—a long shot but certainly possible with the practice I had done.

that the bedded-down ram was more than 800 yards distant, Rick struggled with the rangefinder to get an exact distance. I tried my hand at it and soon had a reading—850 yards. Rick's guess had been accurate.

Rick and Rubin began setting up the other spotting scope and settling in to watch the ram. I was already piling up backpacks to make a rifle rest and got a good look at this ram through my rifle scope. Rick had been right about this bighorn—he was definitely a shooter. Now I was getting really excited. This moment was as thrilling as ever to me. It never seems to lose its excitement.

With my guide and wrangler still setting up, I put the crosshairs on the ram. I concentrated to control my breathing. This would be one of the longest shots at game I had ever taken.

"Let me know before you shoot," Rick said, still setting up the other spotting scope.

I barely heard him. By that time my finger was already tightening on the trigger. The ram had stood up, and he could have been gone in an instant. Rick and Rubin's heads jerked toward me just after my shot cracked.

"I thought you were going to tell me before you shot!" Rick said with some irritation. He later told me that he was concerned that I had shot the wrong ram. As things turned out, I had shot the right one—the biggest in the group.

"I couldn't wait," I said hoping to mollify him. "The ram was starting to move." This was not entirely true. The ram had only stood up. But I wasn't taking any chances.

Rick said that since I had surprised him with the shot, he had no idea where the bullet went. I would later learn that wasn't entirely true. Through the spotting scope, my guide had caught a glimpse of blood on the ram's upper chest as the bighorn began running down the rocky hillside. He withheld this information from me for the time being.

With the ram moving so fast, I assumed my first shot had missed. I was somewhat surprised that the ram was heading to lower ground. That's generally a sign that they've been hit. The other sheep in the group took off in another direction.

By the time the bighorn stopped about 750 yards distant, I had chambered another round. I fired and missed—a low shot. He began running downward and sideways to our position. He stopped again at about 650 yards out. Rick couldn't get the rangefinder working, so a lot of struggling and shouting was going on—some in English, some in Spanish.

In the midst of this pandemonium, the ram began to move again. I fired a couple of more ineffectual rounds—probably high. I lost sight of him as he ran along the side of a slope and parallel to the ridgeline above him.

Rick and Rubin packed up and scurried up the ridge in the direction of the ram below us. I was right behind them. More shouting and chaos. We stopped at the edge of the ridge on a rocky overlook. I caught sight of the bighorn again as he mingled with three other rams on the slopes of a ridge across from and below us. Then I lost him among the cactus and bluffs on the boulder-strewn slope.

We huddled to size up the situation. It was then that Rick told me that he had seen blood on the ram just after my first shot. Being a good psychologist besides a hunting guide, he had not wanted to get me any more excited than I already was. He pointed out a large saguaro on the steep slope and said to look for a cave opening a little to the right of this tall cactus.

"Put your crosshairs on the cave," Rick advised. The opening was about 650 yards distant.

"What am I looking for?" I asked.

"You just keep your crosshairs on that cave," my guide said firmly. Again playing psychologist, Rick didn't want to tell me that he had seen the ram go into the cave. He wanted to calm me down before the action picked up again.

I finally paused long enough to catch my breath. For several exciting minutes I had been breathing heavily from excitement as much as exertion. I had put a lot of lead in the air with little to show for it—but it sure had been fun.

Suddenly the ram stepped from the cave, and my heart began jackhammering in my chest. I shot—and missed again! More chaos and bilingual shouting. Then the bighorn began moving parallel to us and to our left, a flanking move. I fired again to no effect.

He was up and down in the undulating terrain, but mostly horizontal to our position. Then he emerged and slowed on a large, relatively flat patch of yellowish grass. I ranged him at 387 yards. If he continued flanking us, he would soon be around the side of the hill we were on and out of view.

Fighting to stay calm, I set the turret on the scope at 400 yards. The ram began moving again, slowly, still flanking us to the left. I shot again and lost sight of him. I couldn't see where the bullet hit. Neither could Rick. Had we lost him?

Looking through his binoculars, Rubin began shouting excitedly in Spanish. Rick translated: "He's down and dead!"

The three of us began laughing, yelling and high-fiving. As we celebrated, Rick's two-way radio came alive. Some nearby guides wanted to know what all the commotion was about. They heard all the firing and shouting, then the celebration. They said it sounded "like an Afghanistan firefight."

We told them of our success. Raul and Sergio then came on the radio to give us their congratulations. This had been some of the most exciting minutes of hunting I had ever experienced. "How many times did I shoot, Rick?" I asked.

"Five or six," my guide answered. "No wait—three here and four over there. Seven times."

All's well that ends well, but I vowed to myself that the next time I would bring my own rifle on one of these hunts. I had been nearly frantic that this wounded ram would get away. That had already happened on that desert ram hunt near Big Bend National Park. But this Sonoran Desert ram was down and would soon be on his way to my game room. I could hardly have been more thrilled.

We had a difficult maneuver through rough terrain to get to my prize. I took the lead as we came up to the motionless ram, laying on his right side and facing away from us. "Oh, wow! Boy, he's dark," I said walking over to put my hands on his horns.

His deep-brown, uniform coat looked surprisingly clean. I grasped his horns to pull his head up for a better view. "Oh, my gosh, he's got great character," I said, noting the thickness and brooming on

After several of the most exciting minutes I've experienced in my many years of hunting, this magnificent Sonoran darkhorn was headed to my game room.

his sizable horns. The large horns looked oversized compared to his body. We estimated the horns at 155 inches.

"You've just finished up your second Slam, Leonard," Rick said. "Congratulations!"

"I couldn't have done it without you guys," I said sounding a bit trite. But this was absolutely true. It's always a team effort on these kinds of hunts, and everyone shares in the success.

"Look at this," I said rubbing my hand across a large chip at the top of one of his horns. "He's an old warrior."

Inspecting the rings on his horns, my guide estimated the ram to be between nine and twelve years old. Rick pointed out where my first shot had entered and exited the sheep's throat just below his lower jaw. This wound appeared to have done little to slow the sheep and likely would not have been fatal, barring infection. I certainly had not been aiming at the sheep's throat on that long shot, so I had been a little lucky that the slug had struck him where it had. Still, I had no shame in drawing blood at 850 yards with a borrowed rifle.

After photos, we went to work dressing the sheep out in the mid-afternoon sun. Appropriate to the setting, Rick and Rubin worked on the ram between a saguaro cactus to one side and a large organ pipe cactus on the other. The rugged desert terrain in the background extended to the horizon. This broken, rocky landscape resembled areas I had seen inside the Grand Canyon.

As I watched the guide and wrangler work on the ram, the fatigue from the day's efforts set in. We had already hiked more than eight miles through some rough country. Packing this sheep out would only drain us more.

"It'll soon be time for *cervezas* and cigars," I said hoping to boost morale. I barely got a response from the busy skinners.

The sun was setting by the time we packed out. We could barely see the road in the far distance where we would meet our ride back to the ranch house. Heavily loaded, we stumbled along in the dark, crossing through and over rocks, thorns and low cliffs. This was a challenging and exhausting wrap-up to the day's events.

The truck was waiting when we arrived at the roadway. The driver handed me the two beers I had requested over the two-way radio. The celebration was on.

71

North American Desert Sheep Hunting

The festivities continued back at the ranch house, where we were feted with a steak dinner. The deer hunters in camp seemed excited and congratulated me when they saw the ram's head. Outfitter Raul was especially impressed by our success.

After dinner, I went out on the veranda for a beer and cigar. Raul joined me with more compliments on my success. He said not many could have met the physical challenge of this hunt, nor could they have made the 850-yard initial shot. "I am very impressed by your accomplishment,"

Packing out after harvesting my ram was long and arduous, but less so with the deployment of my trusty trekking poles.

he concluded. I thanked him and told him that I had to credit the good Lord above for the health and ability to pull off a hunt like that, and that Rick and Rubin had been invaluable.

Raul may have been laying it on a little thick for his client, but it made me feel pretty good all the same. It had been a helluva day, both wildly exciting and rewarding. I turned in that evening exhausted but looking forward to a mule deer hunt still ahead.

I WAS UP BEFORE DAWN for another lukewarm shower and an omelet breakfast. The demand for hot water exceeded the supply, and I soon learned that only the early bird got the hot shower. We were on the road looking for mule deer before the sun rose.

Our method of deer hunting from the pickup was called "high-rack-ing." Hunters sit or stand in a high rack, which is a kind of elevated cage above the pickup bed. The floor of the rack is level with the top of the cab, providing hunters with a commanding view of the surrounding area. This method is particularly effective in area with heavy ground cover, as the hunters are positioned above this growth. Our high rack was equipped with two swivel chairs. High-racking is sort of like stand hunting in Texas, except that one's stand (higher than the cab of the pickup) is mobile.

I had heard that some hunters in southwest United States use this method to hunt deer, but I had never tried it. Any initial concern about being jolted out of the rack while traveling soon diminished. The rack felt stable, and the truck moved at only moderate speeds.

With Rick driving, Rubin and I stood in the rack looking for deer. We drove the dirt roads to various knobs from which to glass. If we saw quality mule deer from the truck, we could plan our approach.

"High-racking" is a method of hunting deer from an elevated cage on the back of a pickup. Used mostly in areas with heavy ground cover, "high-racking" provides hunters a mobile hunting stand.

If we didn't see deer, we could hike up the higher ground on these knobs and glass the distant terrain.

The temperature was in the mid-50s as the sun began to climb. In this flatter terrain, the desert looked like a giant rock garden with the tall, impassive saguaro and other varieties of cactus rising above the floor in every direction. The expanse of exotic growth looked beautiful in the tranquil morning air, but it could pose a danger to a careless hiker. Still, at least in these lower parts of the Sonoran, we wouldn't have to worry about the dreaded, diarrhea-inducing *"yer-va-flecha"* plants.

I hoped this trip would add a heavy-horned, 30-inch-wide mule deer to my collection. Mule deer had long been a staple in my annual game hunts, but I had never been able to reach that impressive 30-inch horn spread. I was concerned more with the width than the points on one of these mule deer racks. The muleys in this region were noted for their wide horns.

It was nice to stretch my legs on the short jaunts up some of these knobs. With most of the ground covered in the pickup, high-racking was much less strenuous than the sheep hunting of the previous two days. I was happy to give my legs a break. Glassing over the desert floor from the knobs, I was impressed by the panoply of tangled growth. The higher rainfall during the year had the desert floor in full bloom, providing good browsing for the deer and nearly impossible hiking in some areas.

We drove back to the ranch house for a midday break, and there I found Raul out back practicing with his bow—although "practicing" might not be a good word to describe his activity. This guy was a world-class bowman. He was actually breaking airborne clay pigeons with blunt-tipped arrows, just like a shooter at a gun range with a shotgun. This was a truly impressive display of archery skills.

After a burrito lunch, the three of us took a short *siesta* before continuing our high-racking in the afternoon sun. We were seeing mule deer that afternoon, but mostly does. We began the drive back to the ranch house as the sun set over the not-too-distant Sea of Cortez. And it wasn't just an ordinary sunset. The sky seemed to explode in massive streaks of red, yellow and gray. The wind-blown red dirt of western Oklahoma makes for some impressive sunsets, but the late afternoon skies of the western Sonoran Desert are a wonderment to behold.

We viewed one of the other hunter's mule deer that evening at the ranch house. It was a nice specimen, but not the wide rack I hoped for. I soon turned in to get an early start the next day.

Up at four for another unsatisfying, lukewarm shower and a burrito breakfast, by sunup we were again out on the dirt roads high-racking for mule deer. The day started cool and cloudy. Midmorning we came upon a group of muley does, and Rick tried to attract a buck with his deer caller. This high-pitched mating call sounded like the cry of a bird, but failed to bring in one of the wide-horned muley bucks. My guide said this "bleating" call worked really well during the rut, but we were a week or two early on this early-December day.

Midday, our high-racking travels took us to Rancho La Primavera, where Raul held a hunting lease. We parked at the main ranch house to discuss the best deer locations with the owner. Speaking in Spanish, Rick and Rubin engaged in a rapid-fire, in-depth discussion with the rancher while I stood by cluelessly.

The rancher gave good directions to deer locations, and we soon spotted a couple of handsome muley bucks. They were a couple of hundred yards back in some fairly dense growth. We could see them with our binoculars, but they apparently couldn't see us. One of these bucks was impressive. If not for my extensive collection of good mule deer, I would have taken this big forky. Tempting, but he just didn't have the width that I sought.

We were treated to a dinner of spaghetti and sautéed shrimp that evening at the ranch house. Just as satisfying to me was the hot shower that evening. The only sure way to get hot water was to shower when others weren't.

By seven the next morning, we left the pickup on our way up a knob to glass for that elusive 30-inch mule deer. The sun was still below the horizon on this clear, crisp morning, and a full moon hovered just over our knob ahead. This desert moon made a stunning silhouette in the gathering light of dawn.

We bushwhacked our way through heavy growth to the top of the knob. Just as we set up to start glassing, the sun peeked over the desert floor below. The stunning desert scenery in the dawn light was mesmerizing. In the far distance to the northeast I could make out what appeared to be a true mountain range, as opposed to the mostly big, rocky hills and low mountains in Raul's hunting leases. We had a commanding view of the surrounding area, and if necessary Rick wanted to spend a couple of hours here glassing for deer. I hoped that much time wouldn't be necessary, but if so, the outstanding scenery would compensate.

Using the spotting scope, Rubin soon located several muley bucks and does, but none with the wide rack I wanted. Still early in the morning, Rubin also spotted a group of Coues deer. One of these was an excellent Coues buck. "*Muy grande*," the wrangler said. I had never heard the diminutive Coues deer described as "very big," but this buck certainly impressed Rubin.

This smaller subspecies of the white-tailed deer can be found in remote mountains and hills from the southwestern United States into northwestern Mexico. Possibly Arizona's finest game animal, the Coues deer (*Odocoileus virginianus couesi*) of Arizona is indistinguishable from those of the state of Sonora.

I had never before hunted Coues deer. Although drawn for a couple of Coues permits in Arizona, I had passed on these hunts. The undersized white-tails had never had strong appeal to a regular mule deer hunter like me.

Still, I had a Coues deer tag on this hunt in the Sonora, and we might not find that coveted 30-inch mule deer that I so wanted. Plus, the challenge appealed to me. A good Coues deer buck can be hard to find and even harder to bring down. The chase was on to bag this elusive game.

The Coues (properly pronounced as *cows*, but more generally *coos*) deer has a reputation for hiding in even the slightest area of cover and is considered by many to be the most challenging variety of deer to hunt. Often referred to as the "gray ghost," famed hunter and outdoor writer Jack O'Connor called the Coues "the most difficult of all deer to kill" because of its extreme wariness and inhospitable habitat.

Rubin had first spotted this Coues buck at 1,200 yards distant. Deciding to go for it, I got pretty excited as we packed up to relocate. The buck was comfortably bedded in the early morning light, but we were concerned that he might start to move once the sun got higher. Out of view of the buck, we hustled toward a hill closer to where he was bedded. Our approach was directly from east of this deer, so the rising sun would be in his eyes—a big help in avoiding detection by this sharp-eyed critter.

Ranging the buck from our new location, we were still 650 yards out. I had earlier made the 850-yard shot on the desert ram, but I had the benefit of a little luck on that shot. Without my own rifle, I didn't want to attempt another long shot. We spied another hill closer to the still-bedded buck and were again on the move.

With the sun still behind us, we emerged atop the closer knob some 330 yards from the Coues. The buck was below us on the slope of a ridge, which was sparsely covered with saguaro and low bushes. Even with the borrowed rifle, I felt confident at this range. The wind was swirling a bit at about ten to twelve miles per hour. I set the turret on 350 yards.

My pulse accelerated as I looked through the riflescope for the deer. He was no longer bedded. Where was he?

Rick told me he was behind a big saguaro near where he had been bedded. "Just put your crosshairs on that saguaro, Leonard," my guide said.

I did as he advised, but still saw nothing. It seemed like we had played this scene before with the big ram. My guide was once again telling me to keep my crosshairs on something besides the game, which I couldn't even see. I fought to stay calm as the tension mounted.

Then the Coues stepped out from behind the saguaro. I had the crosshairs on him, but some tall brush partly obscured him. This would not be a clean shot. I waited, forcing deep breaths.

The buck took a couple more steps and cleared the bushes. Just behind me, Rick gave a loud whistle. The deer froze, standing broadside. A perfect target and a downhill shot. I put the crosshairs on his shoulder. *Boom!* He dropped in his tracks.

Rick hollered his congratulations and we high-fived. Rubin, who had been positioned far behind us, rapidly came up with a congratulatory hug. Once again I was reminded of the team effort that contributes to this kind of success. Rick had guided us to a likely location for deer, Rubin had spotted the Coues buck, and I had made the shot. Everyone played a role.

Rick kept his binoculars on the downed buck and seemed impressed with this specimen. "Looks pretty good even from this distance," my guide said. "Even down on the ground I can see the super-wide rack. That's a good Coues."

I suppose it's all relative, but I hardly thought of this miniature specimen of white-tail as having a "super-wide rack." It may have been wide for a Coues deer, but the 30-inch muley horns I still hoped to claim would dwarf this rack. Still, Rick was right to call this a fine specimen of a Coues buck. It would be nice to have a full-sized mount of this inhabitant of the Sonoran Desert. I was pleased and excited.

We hiked over to the deer. "Little bitty guy," I said getting a full view of the buck.

I had come to Sonora primarily for one of their celebrated darkhorn rams, but this handsome Coues deer turned out to be a nice bonus from this adventure.

"About the same size as an antelope," Rick added. "A little gray ghost."

"Look how dark his horns are," I said. The darker horns of deer and elk usually come from their rubbing against pine trees in the higher elevations. I was unsure why the Coues in this region had dark horns—a genetic trait perhaps.

Rick and Rubin examined the buck as I stepped back to record the scene with my camcorder. Although pint-sized, this Coues was truly a handsome little fellow. "He's got a nice bow, good forks," I noted. "Good brow tines. He is a classic, isn't he?" The more I looked, the more I liked.

"He's a beautiful little guy," Rick added, perfectly describing this Coues specimen. My guide estimated that this mature buck would weigh around ninety pounds.

After the deer was dressed out, Rick and I packed out the head, hide and quarters to the road not far below while Rubin walked back to get the truck. By late morning the temperature was rising, so we would need to get this meat in a cooler.

I lit up a cigar while sitting in the rack on our return to the ranch house. This had been my fifth day of hunting on this trip, and a desert bighorn and Coues deer were in the bag. I still had four days left to take that wide muley.

We were back at the ranch house early, so I beat the other hunters to a hot shower. The others returned late in the day with little to show for their efforts. My little Coues deer got most of the attention. That evening Rick scored him at 101 points. A Boone and Crockett Coues is 110, so my little guy provided a good representation of this species.

We were out hunting mule deer before sunrise the next morning, bumping along the private roads of a couple of area ranches. The roads maintained by the ranchers were distinctly better than the state-maintained roads. The morning was cool, but the rising sun rapidly warmed the desert air.

Not seeing mule deer from the rack, we parked the truck and hiked half mile or so up a steep knob. This position gave us great views in all directions. We didn't see deer below us, but we did find a striking Sonoran Desert tortoise right at the top of this knob. It seemed strange that he would make his living at this height, and I could only imagine how difficult his climb up this steep knob must have been.

The next three days weren't much different than the previous. The muley bucks were scarce. We high-racked, exited the truck to glass from higher ground, and moved on. We ventured out on one of the more remote ranches in the area, and some of the roads had fallen into neglect. We occasionally stopped to repair the road before proceeding, and even got stuck in a deep rut on one occasion.

I would miss out on a mule deer on this trip, but I did have that trophy Coues deer as a consolation prize. And I had a remarkable desert bighorn to add to my ever-growing game room in Oklahoma. This successful ram hunt had also secured my second Grand Slam of North American wild sheep. Moreover, this adventure had been filled with unforgettable scenes of rock, plant life and sky, a landscape fitting for an artist's canvas. Memories of these striking desert vistas would be mine forever.

I was already planning a return to this wild region. My week in the Sonoran had left me wanting more—not just a prized desert muley, but a challenging hunt for another desert bighorn. This outdoor experience had been one of my most memorable, even after decades of quests for North American game in other wild and scenic regions. While visiting this unique region, I had looked on with awe at the colors on the western horizon and marveled at the jungle of plant life. What a stately sight the silent saguaro had made jutting above the desert floor, mingling with the rocky hills, and the waters of the gulf as the sun set on the Sonoran Desert.

CHAPTER 4

A Weems Hunt in the
Sierra de la Giganta
(2018)

Planning a trip to the Wild Sheep Foundation's 2017 Sheep Show in Reno, Nevada, my thoughts turned to completing my third Grand Slam of Wild Sheep. I only needed a third Rocky Mountain bighorn and a third desert bighorn to attain this distinction.

Since I had already taken a Mexican and a Nelson desert ram, I was looking to book a hunt for a Weems ram (*Ovis canadensis weemsi*), or perhaps a Peninsular ram (*Ovis canadensis cremnobates*), on the exotic Baja California peninsula. Most of the Baja peninsula is remote and physically challenging for hunters. As do all wild sheep, these desert critters reside in secluded areas, which on this peninsula are even more wild and exceptional, and difficult to access. Once you get close to the sheep, it can be more like a typical hunt. But packing into those high, tropical-desert reaches can be a feat in itself. And living there for a few days of eating, sleeping, and enduring can be a wholly different challenge.

While at the February convention in the Reno-Sparks Convention Center, I signed a contract with the renowned Bo Morgan's outfit for a Weems sheep hunt. It would be a pack-in hunt in the remote highlands west of the seaside town of Loreto in Baja California Sur, the Mexican state on the lower end of the peninsula. Morgan's GoWithBo Booking and Guide Service specializes in sheep and goat hunts worldwide.

North American Desert Sheep Hunting

It took me nearly a year to obtain the required permits for the sheep and to import my Gunwerks rifle. Fortunately, Bo Morgan's wife, Jerrin, helped me with this. When it comes to firearms, Mexican government officials can be even more bureaucratic than the Canadians, whom I had dealt with many times before. So by early February 2018, I planned to be on my way from Oklahoma City to Loreto via Los Angeles International Airport (LAX). I added a black-tail deer (*Odocoileus hemionus columbianus)* permit to this hunt since the region is noted for this subspecies of mule deer.

A lot of planning and physical conditioning went into this adventure. In the months before the hunt, I went to my fitness center about six days a week mixing a variety of aerobic and strength-training exercises. I worked with a trainer to build up my legs and combined these workouts with bicycle training. In the weeks leading up to the hunt, I completed some trail runs wearing my hiking boots.

Although I had experienced generally good results with my Gunwerks LR-1200 rifle for a number of years, a few months before the Baja hunt I discovered that the rounds were not cycling in the magazine. I shipped the rifle back to Gunwerks for a fix, but after its return I continued to have the same problem. So I would be on this sheep hunt with a single-shot firearm. Not ideal.

I hoped to mitigate this deficiency in my rifle by improving my long-range accuracy. Shooting game at more than 300 yards was actually fairly routine for me as I practiced diligently at long-distance shooting. But I determined to get even better for this hunt. After frequent trips to the firing range on my ranch in the Texas Panhandle, I felt dead-on at 500 to 700 yards. If all worked as planned, my single-shot rifle would suffice.

After decades of hunting throughout North America, my collection of outdoor gear was extensive, but for this hunt I tailored my gear to the "tropical-desert climate" in the mountains of Baja California Sur. This meant concentrating on light-weight, thermal-efficient clothing and sleeping gear like that made by KUIU. I had learned what did *not* work just the year before on an elk hunt in the mountains of Colorado. A well-known national brand looked sharp but utterly failed in the thermal-efficiency department.

On the other hand, the KUIU gear I wore on this fall hunt worked

My Weems sheep hunt in Baja California Sur would bring me to the seaside village of Loreto, which nestles along the west coast of the peninsula between the Sea of Cortez and the exotic Sierra de la Giganta range, as shown above.

to perfection. The "technical layering system" for KUIU's outdoor apparel kept me warm even while perspiring in the cool, low-humidity altitudes of the Rocky Mountains. (I receive nothing from KUIU for speaking well of their products; I'm just providing experience-driven advice to other hunters and outdoorsmen.)

For a February 2018 hunt in the mountains of the Baja peninsula, I prepared for temperatures between 50 and 70 degrees during the day and around 40 degrees at night. Since we would be packing into a spike camp, I wanted a light-weight (around two-pound) sleeping bag rated at zero degrees. Bo Morgan helped me get a good deal on a KUIU sleeping bag at the January 2018 Sheep Show, where I was displaying my first book.

While at this exhibition, I also renewed my membership in Global Rescue Travel Services, a safety precaution that Morgan recommends. Membership with the service provides a no-hassles evacuation in remote areas in the event of an accident, sickness, or political turmoil. Just as important, this provides peace of mind for a hunter already stressed out with the rigors and challenges of a difficult hunt in harsh conditions. If necessary, Global Rescue will send in a team to extract you and get you where you need to be.

At 11:30 THE MORNING OF FEBRUARY 7, a taxi dropped me off at Oklahoma City's Will Rogers World Airport. Flying with 91 pounds of gear and with no skycap to aid me, I confiscated a large cart that said "Not for Public Use" to get my bags to check-in. I got through security with little hassle as I had done a pre-check with TSA the day before. My travel agent had upgraded my flight to first-class status, well worth the extra expense in my estimation.

I made it to LAX on schedule, and again with no skycaps available, I pirated a cart to tow my bags to the pick-up area. A shuttle from the Hilton near the airport delivered me to my lodging for the night. So far so good.

My flight to Loreto was scheduled to depart at 10:30 a.m., but I arrived at LAX hours earlier to ensure plenty of time to check my rifle and ammunition with TSA. Possibly detecting gun powder residue on me or my gear, the TSA officials patted me down before boarding. All things considered, I made it on board my flight to

Loreto with minimal stress. I knew that the real aggravation still lay ahead with the Mexican officials at the airport in Loreto.

Baja California Sur (Lower California South) encompasses roughly the southern half of the Baja peninsula. With 800,000 inhabitants, it is the least populated but ninth largest in area of the thirty-one Mexican states. BC Sur is also the newest Mexican state, changing its status from territory to statehood in October 1974. Bordered on the east by the Gulf of California and on the west by the Pacific Ocean, the state's most prominent city is the popular tourist resort of Los Cabos on the southern tip of the peninsula.

Our plane touched down around 2:30 p.m. at the airport in Loreto, in northern BC Sur, where I was greeted by my outfitter Eduardo Canett and his wrangler Juan. Eduardo spoke good English and would help me get through customs. Regulations for bringing firearms and ammunition into Mexico are exacting and demanding. After a two-hour wait while the other passengers cleared customs, Mexican officials from both customs and the military began

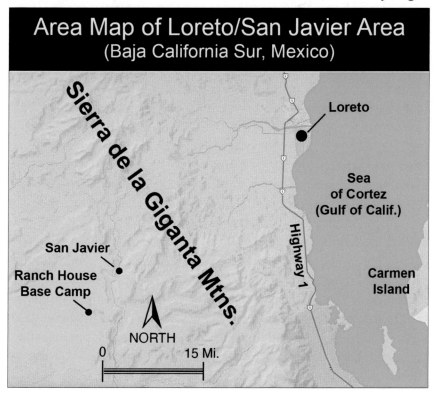

to inspect my rifle, ammunition and paperwork.

All sixty of the bullets I brought along were carefully counted. Flying out after the hunt, I would have to account for each round with either unused bullets or empty shell casings. My rifle and ammunition were carefully photographed and documented. The permits for the firearm and for hunting a wild sheep and a black-tailed deer were scrutinized. Any violation of these regulations could mean a heavy fine.

Considering the rampant gun violence just below the U.S. border, it seems paradoxical that most Mexicans are officially allowed only a firearm permit for a .22-caliber rifle or pistol. Obtaining a rifle with real firepower requires locals to join a hunting or shooting organization, among other bureaucratic hoops to clear. Just goes to show how ineffective gun restrictions are when laws against criminals are lax or unenforced.

Thankfully clearing customs with little drama, we left the airport in Eduardo's late-model silver pickup pulling a trailer with several horses inside. The surrounding scenery was stunning. Loreto hugs the eastern coast of the peninsula along the shore of the gulf. The peaks and ridges of the Sierra de la Giganta mountain range dominate the horizon just to the west of the coastline. The highest point along this range, El Cerro de la Giganta, looms like a colossus 3,900 feet above sea level and just west of Loreto.

We meandered southwesterly on rough, unpaved roadway gaining altitude as we made our way toward the rocky ridges and ravines where the wild sheep roam. Bumping along the dusty roadway for about an hour, we came to the little village of San Javier, less than thirty miles from Loreto. The site is noted for the historic Mission San Javier, founded by Jesuits of the Roman Catholic Church in 1699. The striking mission church was completed in 1754 and is considered the crown jewel of the string of Spanish mission churches built over the centuries along the Baja California peninsula.

The walled structure looks its years but still functions as a church for the locals with a priest from Loreto visiting every fifteen days. The old bell is rung to call the faithful to mass, a long-standing ritual that dates back several hundred years. We stopped at the ancient church to look around, and I noted what was to me a novelty—orange

The historic Mission San Javier, more than 300 years old, is considered the crown jewel of the Spanish mission churches along the Baja California peninsula.

trees. I certainly don't see those in Oklahoma, but I soon learned that they are plentiful in the foothills of the Sierra de la Giganta.

With less than 200 inhabitants, not much was going on in dusty San Javier that afternoon. Yet I was impressed with the neatness and tidiness of the village. Besides the orange trees, the area was interspersed with healthy-looking palm and other deciduous trees.

North American Desert Sheep Hunting

The palm leaves in the area provided the covering for the *nipa* roofs in the scattered houses and buildings. Except for the visitors' trucks and cars, the village could have been the backdrop for a Clint Eastwood spaghetti Western.

Late in the afternoon we took a rough, unpaved road south from Loreto, continuing upward in the foothills of the Sierra de la Giganta range. We were headed to our chief guide's ranch, a dozen or more miles southwest of San Javier and which would serve as our base camp. The going was slow with torturous, rocky stream crossings. I was surprised we didn't have a flat tire or two. The outlying terrain was generally dusty and arid-looking. Eduardo said the primary crop in the area was garlic. Along the way, we picked up chief guide Francisco, a grizzled 60-year-old local who had been chaperoning hunters in the area since he was 15.

An hour or so before sunset we arrived at Francisco's ranch, which would serve as our base camp. The sound of bleating goats greeted us. The animals' plaintive calls sounded like crying children to me, somewhat creepy at first. Unloading my gear from the truck, I was introduced to wrangler Beto, who would be the fourth member of our hunting party.

Steep cliffs surrounded the small ranch, and a nearby wide creek snaked through the rugged highlands providing water for the household and guests. Our base camp was certainly rustic. Still, it could be considered a luxury compared to many of the camps I have endured. Prepared by Francisco's wife and another woman at the ranch, our sumptuous dinner consisted of flank steak, refried beans, tortillas, guacamole and roasted habaneros. Truly a classic Mexican feast!

Worn out by the day's travel, I turned in early, spreading my sleeping bag in one of the small guest tents under an open-air, *nipa*-covered shelter. My new KUIU sleeping bag worked well. I slept soundly in the cool night air.

Up by 5 a.m., I went through the usual struggle of dressing and packing in a small tent. The sound of bleating goats the evening before had been replaced with the loud hum of a gasoline-powered generator providing electricity to our base camp. The women at base camp served a hearty breakfast.

Afterward, I zeroed in my rifle with a few practice rounds before

Francisco's wife and some of the other ladies at our base camp kept us well fed when we were not in the field, a real luxury I had not expected.

leaving for spike camp. The four rounds at 340 yards were off about three to four inches, disappointing considering all of my recent, long-distance practice. But a downed ram wouldn't know I was off by a few inches, I reckoned.

Our caravan to spike camp left before 9 a.m. Several mounted guides leading horses and mules trailed Eduardo's pickup as we made our way along the increasingly rocky, hazardous road. We would drive the truck until the roadway gave out, then ride the rest of the way to spike camp. We navigated numerous creek crossings, usually preceded by our relocating heavy rocks that had tumbled onto the ford during heavy rains. The truck's creeping over these rocky stretches was a nail-biting ordeal. The rubber ply on the truck tires was the heaviest available, no doubt preventing numerous flats.

Coming to the end of the road, we packed our gear and supplies onto the horses, a mule, and a burro, and began the four-hour ride to spike camp. Ridges and cliffs broke the horizon in every direction, and between the high ground was a jungle of scraggly deciduous trees and various cacti. The temperature was a pleasant 75 to 80 degrees, which I thought surprisingly warm for early February, even in these southern latitudes.

Eduardo said we would be hunting on Francisco's ranch of some 10,000 *hectares*, which translated to around 25,000 acres. This vast expanse was allowed only one permit for a wild sheep that year. *And I'm the lucky hunter that has it*, I thought to myself.

My outfitter had put me on a small horse with good tack. I moseyed along comfortably behind Francisco on the four-hour ride to spike camp with the rest of the pack train and guides behind. The trail followed the same creek that provided water for the base camp now miles behind us. The horsemanship and tack of the guides and wranglers were impressive. These were seasoned *vaqueros.*

Late morning, our caravan stopped in a heavily shaded area for a break. The soaring cliffs and rock palisades around us reminded me

The rocky desert terrain between the high ridges and slopes was the usual mix of cactus and scraggly vegetation.

of areas in West Texas. Despite the region's scanty rainfall, runoff from the higher elevations promotes jungle-like growth around the creeks and washes. Most of the Baja California peninsula lies within the Sonoran Desert, but the runoff-fed vegetation in the higher elevations is much like the tropical thornscrub of the state of Sonora, just across the Gulf of California in Mexico's northwest mainland. Thornscrub includes a complex mixture of low thorn-bearing trees and shrubs, along with a diverse mixture of succulents, including cacti. The statuesque saguaro is ubiquitous in the foothills of the Sierra de la Giganta range.

Scrutinizing this terrain as I munched a burrito on the late-morning lunch break, I felt the building excitement of the hunt. This colorful region was unlike anywhere I had hunted in North America. With only Eduardo speaking passable English, a language barrier separated me from my four *compadres* on this hunt—but that just added to the novelty of this experience. I was pumped and ready for whatever came next.

What came next was another tough couple of hours in the saddle and walking our horses several times on steep ascents. This was probably the roughest horseback ride I've ever had. At one point Francisco's horse stumbled in a rocky crevasse, and I thought it had broken its leg.

After exactly four hours of riding, we arrived at our spike camp, dropping our gear on a relatively flat saddle within a rocky, cactus-covered landscape. The campsite appeared to be in one of the few relatively level spaces in the area. An established fire pit told me this spike camp had been used many times before.

We would use the remaining daylight to glass for sheep on higher ground and finish setting up camp at dusk. Before leaving, we took a snack break. I looked back at the bend in a faraway canyon from where we had come. Our campsite was on a broad saddle in a very remote expanse, perched on steep, sloping landscape surrounded by high cliffs and pinnacles. Eating a fresh-picked orange, I watched the tethered horses grazing for whatever they could find in the thin grasses of this rocky saddle.

Around 2 p.m. our party split in several directions to glass a broader area of sheep country. I was grateful to have my trekking

Our spike camp was on a broad saddle surrounded by the soaring pinnacles of the Sierra de la Giganta ranges. The well-established fire pit testified to the many times this site had been used by hopeful hunters.

poles to pull myself up on the area's steep slopes. I nestled in among some rocks and began glassing the cliffs and ridges below. But the magnificent scenery distracted me from the hunt. To the east, the turquoise expanse of the Gulf of California glimmered in the late afternoon sunlight. I studied the western coastline of elongated Carmen Island, which extends north to south for a dozen miles or so. With a spine of low mountains providing hideouts and escape routes, the island has been the home of a repopulation program for desert sheep since 1995.

To the northwest of Carmen Island, I could make out the outline of tiny Coronado Island. With its white sandy beaches, the island get-away is only a half-hour boat ride from Loreto, where I had flown in just a day earlier. Closer to my rocky roost where I was supposed to be glassing for sheep, I could make out the distant outline of some of the buildings in Loreto. From my position to the southwest, the town lay between Coronado Island and the northern tip of Carmen Island.

When not distracted by this incredible scenery, I was able to spot three ewes and one small ram along the distant cliffsides below. These few and distant sheep were not nearly as exciting as the scenery. Before hiking back down to our campsite, I took in the deep canyons and high cliffs. Dark shadows gathered in this rocky, broken expanse of landscape. With growing apprehension, I was beginning to appreciate the incredibly rugged terrain in this region. Maneuvering through these canyons and over these ridges was going to pose a challenge.

I joined the rest of the hunting party to finish setting up camp pitching our tents as the sun set. The rest of the group had spotted only the same ewes and immature ram that I had seen. I made my bed in the tent with four saddle blankets and a one-pound air mattress. My KUIU sleeping bag would keep me snug in the cool, dry night air.

The outlying areas from our spike camp spoke of the exotic and treacherous terrain we would have to confront in our quest for wild sheep. These surroundings were both intimidating and exhilarating.

North American Desert Sheep Hunting

After a quick dinner, I crawled into my tent a little after 7 p.m. and reviewed the day's events—the rough horse ride to spike camp and the brutal terrain I was just getting acquainted with. I knew this could turn into one of the toughest adventures of my five decades of hunting. In the morning we would split up again and hike deeper into the surrounding canyons and cliffs. It would be even harder climbing and bushwhacking as we glassed for sheep. I had put in a lot of physical training while preparing for this adventure. As I lay in my tent that evening, I could only hope my conditioning would be enough.

I was up by 5:00. Struggling in the low tent to get dressed and packed for the day ahead, I heard the others begin to stir. Making my way to the campfire, I was served a bean *empanada* for breakfast. This Mexican delicacy consists of pinto beans and sugar cooked to a paste, then spread over a warm tortilla. I added a little powdered chocolate to my coffee, providing a crude mocha beverage to my breakfast. My *compadres* heartily approved of this spike-camp luxury.

Before we broke camp and began glassing, I put out a small solar blanket to help us recharge our cell phones, flashlights and other battery-powered devices. Everyone in the group would put this recharging system to good use.

Francisco, Juan and Beto soon took off for higher ground to begin glassing. Eduardo and I initially moved to a higher position near our campsite. After failing to spot sheep, Eduardo went to another area while I relocated just above camp. Sitting alone on the saddle—again with that eye-popping view toward the gulf to the east—I spent all morning glassing and sucking up the scenery. It was rugged and beautiful, but the rugged part continued to worry me some. How would we get through this maze of rocks and cliffs below us to get to any sheep we spied in the distance? Then, how could we possibly get the horns, hide and meat out if I were fortunate enough to shoot one of these exotic bighorns?

When I had expressed these concerns to Eduardo earlier, he nonchalantly replied, *"No hay problema."* If I shot a ram, retrieval would not be a problem, he assured.

Later in the morning, I had a nice lunch of cold fried chicken.

94

As our party glassed for sheep in the intimidating maze of cliffs and rocks, I began to worry about how we would retrieve a downed sheep in this jumble of treacherous terrain. My guide, however, expressed no concerns.

Sitting in the saddle was comfortable, and a breeze around 10 miles per hour held steady. A mountain pass or saddle like this almost always came with a breeze, I remembered. I wasn't seeing sheep, but I looked through my gear for my rangefinder just in case. Disgustedly, I realized Eduardo was carrying it, and he was nowhere in sight. This could be a big problem for me if opportunity knocked.

And it did, of course. Around 2:30, Francisco, Juan and Beto excitedly came down to my position on the rocks. "Leonardo, *beeg* deer. *Muy grande!*" Francisco conveyed in broken English. The guide led me to a higher position and pointed to an area far below. I couldn't see the deer with my binoculars, and I didn't have my rangefinder in any event. I was stymied.

One of the wranglers was able to reach Eduardo by short-wave radio. From the other side of our mountain, my outfitter talked the situation over with Francisco. Francisco communicated to me that he calculated the black-tailed deer was some 350 yards out. We moved to get a better view, and I finally spotted the buck. He looked

95

good and was bedded down near a large, flat rock that looked almost white on top. I had a permit for a deer with the one for a wild sheep.

I felt lost without my rangefinder, but got into a prone position among a pile of rocks on a nearby overlook. I chambered one round in my "single-shot" rifle, still handicapped by this bullet-cycling problem with the magazine. The sun was behind me, and I could only see black through my scope. I turned down the power magnification and adjusted the relief between my eye and the scope opening. Problem solved.

Still, without the rangefinder, this shot was a SWAG ("scientific, wild-ass guess" in military parlance). Getting my breathing under control, I put the crosshairs on him a little high, and slowly...slowly...squeezed the trigger. Before I could assess the result, the guide and wranglers began shouting and jumping excitedly. *The deer was down!* I couldn't believe it!

After a brief celebration, we calmed ourselves. Communicating as best he could, Francisco asked me if I wanted to go down with them to retrieve my prize. I looked down the steep, rocky slopes below and asked if this was required. "*No mas, no mas,*" he replied. *No more, no more,* I translated to myself. Maybe it had been a requirement of hunters in this area at one time, but no longer was.

I certainly had no interest in battling my way down the rocky slope to that downed deer. I slowly shook my head side to side. "No way," I said unequivocally. Understanding my English perfectly, all three laughed.

I found a comfortable seat to watch the trio picking their way down the slopes and tangle of rocks and growth to the deer below. It may have been only 350 yards to the deer as the crow flies, but it would require at least a half mile of brutal scrambling to get to him. After some time, Eduardo arrived with my rangefinder. After a brief discussion, my outfitter began struggling down to the others to oversee the skinning of the black-tail for a life-sized mount.

I ranged the downed buck as they worked on him. The instrument told me it was 307 yards to the deer, with a true ballistics range (TBR) of 230 yards after compensation for the downward angle. I had set my bullet-drop compensator at 350 yards, so I had been fortunate to down that deer. *I think I'll start leaving my rangefinder at home*, I joked to myself.

Around 6 p.m. they made it back up to me with the hide, horns and meat. It had been a tough climb for them, and they had used ropes to pull up the cliffsides. I couldn't help but chuckle to myself as I watched them sweating profusely as they rested on some rocks.

"He's still young," Eduardo said as we looked the buck over. "He's probably between three and a half or four." My outfitter explained how the deer in these forage-starved mountains rarely grew large.

"He's not bad," I said. He was actually a great representative of

I had come to the Baja peninsula primarily for a Weems ram, but this trophy black-tailed deer would come first on this hunt.

his species and scored well enough to qualify as a trophy black-tailed deer. We had venison that evening, seasoned with lime and salt. It gave the meat a somewhat sweet taste.

While eating dinner we made plans for the next day. We would continue to glass this area in the morning, but if no shootable rams were spotted by noon, we would pack out to where we had left the truck the day before and move to another location on the ranch. Turning in that evening, the wind had really picked up. Our colorful tents swayed in the breeze.

WE WERE UP BY 5:00 eating warmed-over venison for breakfast. Everyone went in different directions, agreeing to meet back in camp by noon if no good rams were seen. I went back to my perch not too far above camp.

Around 10:30, Eduardo and Juan climbed up to my position. Francisco had spotted seven rams in the distance and below my position. One looked good. We set up the spotting scope to study them, but they began moving around a distant pinnacle. They were miles away and the terrain between was steeply downhill and broken. If we tried to close the gap, it would take most of a very hard day to get within shooting range. Moreover, we probably wouldn't be able to get back up the steep slopes to our campsite. We would have to pack out in a different direction.

We continued to watch the rams through the spotting scope. One was definitely nice. They ambled around to the other side of the pinnacle. We continued watching to see if they came back into view. If they did, or maybe even if they didn't, we would leave early in the morning to stalk them. It would be so steep in places that we would need ropes to descend. Sensing my unease, Eduardo assured me the party would go slow through this brutal terrain.

Mid-afternoon we all went back to our campsite to pack the deer meat on a horse. Beto would take the meat and horses back to meet another rider bringing food and water. The rider would take the meat out, and Beto would water our horses and return that evening with the fresh supplies.

Using the spotting scope, we kept trying to locate the sheep in the distance. But as the sun sat behind us, no sheep. We reviewed our plans to descend the steep terrain the next day and get within range of the rams' presumed position. It would be a tough day ahead. We turned in early.

The camp came alive again at 5:00. We ate quickly, packed up, and said goodbye to our comfortable spike camp. We had the long ride from hell ahead and wouldn't be returning to this site. Eduardo estimated about eight hours of riding, hiking and bushwhacking to get into position on a saddle overlooking the sheep's position. We were all praying the sheep would stay close to the pinnacle where we had seen them the day before.

I had never ridden in such tough conditions. We bushwhacked steeply downward through a jungle of scraggly desert thornscrub, boulders and ravines. We had to dismount frequently and lead the horses through some of the more dangerous passages. It was unnerving and exhausting for horses and riders.

We stopped late in the morning for an early lunch. I was getting attached to the exotic bean *empanadas*, finding them tasty and probably healthy—at least healthier than the greasy refried beans of the Tex-Mex restaurants in Oklahoma. After lunch, more bushwhacking until we finally reached the floor of the canyon. The trail got a little easier in this flatter terrain.

Early afternoon we came to a spring surrounded by palm trees. This was not unlike a classic desert oasis excepting the backdrop of steep rocky cliffs and ridges instead of sand dunes. The spring was a welcome sight in this dry landscape and a good place to take a break. Our mounts got a good watering.

By late afternoon we were on the saddle overlooking the area where we had spotted the sheep. We were probably about five miles from our earlier spike camp, as the crow flies. Almost eight hours of zig-zag scrambling to relocate only five miles from our earlier position!

We split up and began glassing. By 5 p.m. none of us had spotted the rams. We decided to set up our spike camp before dark. Despite not seeing the sheep, we believed they were in the vicinity. The wind was blowing toward where we thought the sheep were bedded, so we had to make do with a cold camp. No fire, cold chicken for our entrée, and no after-dinner cigars.

This desert oasis was not unlike one that could be found in the arid lands of the Arabian Peninsula. It was a welcome relief and great place to water our thirsty stock.

Up at 6:00. This was our fifth day in the field, and we were still hunting for a Weems ram. I had a nice black-tailed deer to show for my efforts, but I had come here primarily for the ram. I hadn't been shut out on a sheep hunt like this in many years. After fighting through this torturous terrain, our hunting party deserved better.

By 8:00 we were seeing sheep, but all ewes and small rams. None of the more mature males we had seen two days earlier. Eduardo, Juan and I rode into a nearby canyon to get different views of the area.

Around mid-morning Francisco radioed that he had spotted three good-looking rams. They were about a three-hour scramble from us, and it would be a long-distance shot once in position. I was feeling a little frustrated and felt like we needed to make a play. We decided to go for those distant rams.

As usual for this area, the hiking and riding was brutal. Francisco led the way with his machete, bushwhacking through the steep, rocky passages. I tried riding one of the pack mules, but after the first 100 yards, I dismounted. The ride was too steep to stay on the beast. I would rather hike. Eduardo walked behind to brace me if I slipped on the steep cliffsides. The near vertical slopes occasionally required us to use ropes for ascending and descending. I hadn't rappelled like this in many years—nor had I wanted to. Sometimes you just "do what you gotta do" to get to wild sheep.

After a couple of hours of this extreme workout, we stopped on a steep, rocky outcropping, and Francisco radioed Beto, who was above and far behind us with the spotting scope. The rams were about where we thought they were, Beto said, but we were now out

Beyond the brutal terrain we glassed and traversed, the placid waters of the Sea of Cortez made for a beautiful backdrop.

of position. We needed to backtrack about a mile and move farther around the mountain.

This unwelcome news was followed by more bushwhacking, rappelling, and sliding on the steep slopes. This was exhausting and occasionally frightening. I was grateful I had done so much physical preparation for this hunt. I was hanging by a thread—but still hanging. I had more years on me than any of my tough *compadres*, so I took a grudging satisfaction in staying in this hunt. But I kept thinking this might be the last of my dangerous and difficult hunting challenges—which for the past few years had been my usual musings when grinding through one of these outdoor ordeals.

After moving around the mountain and working our way up, we carefully peered over the ridge. Two mature rams were below us more than 500 yards distant. Despite our cautiousness, the wary critters kept looking in our direction. They either saw, smelled, heard or just sensed our presence. I studied them with my binoculars. They were both really good! My pulse quickened.

I moved to a comfortable position and built a rest for my rifle with our backpacks. My rangefinder said 515 yards—which should be nearly a chip shot considering my recent practice at 600 to 800 yards. As I chambered a round, I heard Eduardo's fierce whisper: *"Leonardo, don't shoot!"*

The older ram had moved in front of the younger one. Not good. My shot could pass through both sheep. It would be inadvertent—but still could be expensive and punitive. I waited.

Slowly adjusting my rifle, I kept one eye on the rams. I finally saw some separation between the pair, but the more mature one in front was now directly facing me. Not an ideal shot. I held the crosshairs on the front of the ram's chest, hoping he would turn a little. I heard Eduardo tell me to wait until he turned broadside.

Holding the crosshairs on his chest, I considered the situation as I waited on my target to turn...even just a little. I had ranged this ram carefully, I had a good firm rest. This was a straightforward shot. The ram was frozen...still facing me...immobile...Sphinx-like. *I'm ready to bring this adventure to a close*, I thought to myself as my finger tightened on the trigger.

The crash of my rifle broke the stillness. A puff of dirt kicked up just beyond the rams. *A clear miss! Impossible! Damn!*

I just couldn't believe it. I had been practicing at targets hundreds of yards farther out with consistent success. I felt like I couldn't miss at 500 yards? But I had. Both animals were up and running hard.

Francisco and Eduardo's eyes met mine and locked. A look of dismay spread across each of our faces. To say I felt down was an understatement, more like crushed...and embarrassed. We had endured pure misery to get into position on this shooter, and I had muffed it. Disgusting! More misery lay ahead if we continued this hunt.

Eduardo broke the gloomy silence when he radioed Beto to see if the rams were still in the vicinity. We held out hope that they had run a short distance and stopped to look back. Sheep will sometimes do that. But Beto said they were still running. Bad news. *Probably run for the rest of the day*, I groused silently, still kicking myself.

But wait! Beto also had some good news. He had spotted another good-looking ram back toward our spike camp. This *was* good news—and bad news. We would have to backtrack through the same wretched terrain we had fought through all morning. Ugh! Still, I was surprised and thankful for the news about this ram. It helped put my recent failure out of mind.

So we were off again in the early afternoon—bushwhacking, scrambling, climbing and sweating up and down the slopes as we worked our way back. We soon began clambering up higher ground, so I was using the ropes more pulling up than rappelling down.

After making it back to where we had tethered our mule and burro earlier in the morning, I tried riding the burro to save my rubbery legs. But as before, the going was just too steep. The burro and I could end up sliding down the side of the mountain. Years earlier, I had a sliding experience riding a horse on a tree blowdown in Canada. I felt fortunate to have escaped injury from a rollover. No use pressing my luck now.

In truth, I was also feeling my years. The past ten years or so I had enjoyed the luxury of taking more time away from my businesses and indulging my passion for hunting in wild and scenic places. I had pounded over and across the mountains, glaciers, ridgelines and deserts of North America—from the Arctic Circle of Alaska to the thornscrub of Sonora and now on the Baja California peninsula.

I had put a lot of miles on my legs while hunting and preparing for these hunts. Wild sheep hunting in rugged, remote hideouts was especially challenging. My body was telling me this might be my last hunt for an elusive bighorn ram.

Guided by Beto on the radio, we moved into position above the ram in mid-afternoon. I finally located him with my binoculars. This solo mature ram was in the area above camp we had glassed earlier that morning. I was thoroughly exhausted from battling up and down this tropical-desert terrain. But I had another chance to bring this hunt to a close. My previous disappointment and bone-weariness were forgotten.

I maneuvered onto a rocky point giving me a broad view of the area where the ram was browsing in the distance above me. I began setting up, keeping one eye on my quarry. I ranged him at 415 yards. I stretched out in a prone position deploying the bipod affixed to me rifle. This felt like a perfect rest. My rifle was rock solid. I had already put my earlier miss out of mind. I thought only of the many times I had just recently hit a bull's-eye at this range.

"He's not a *beeg* one," I heard Eduardo whisper behind me, "but he's *leegal*."

After all I had endured the last couple of days, he was plenty big for me and a fine specimen of a Weems sheep. He was facing slightly to my right, not broadside but a good target. Controlling my breathing, I willed my aching body to relax. I put the crosshairs just behind his right shoulder and began tightening my finger on the trigger.

Everything felt right...I continued tightening on the trigger. The rifle jolted my shoulder as the shot crashed in the mid-afternoon stillness. This time the bullet did the job. The ram barely moved before toppling to the ground. *That's one dead ram*, I thought to myself, *not a big one, but legal and handsome.*

I heard my *compadres* shouting in celebration behind me. This was a much different scene than the gloomy silence that had followed my earlier miss that day. What a turnabout—and all within a few hours! I don't know if I've ever experienced such a low and such a high that close together while hunting.

Just goes to show how quickly things can change when hunting wild sheep, or any game for that matter. You have to keep your chin up and stay alert for new opportunities no matter how disappointed you may be feeling after missing a shot. Opportunities can come and go in a flash.

As I continued viewing the still ram through my binoculars, Eduardo congratulated me and asked if I wanted to hike up and take photos. "Hell no!" I stated emphatically. "I'll stay at the ridge." I requested they bring the ram up to the ridge crest where we had first viewed him. We could take photos there.

The downed ram was only a little over 400 yards distant, but the cliffs and ridges between me and my prize would take close to an hour for us to ascend. Not for me—nor for the 60-year-old guide sitting beside me. Francisco had struggled over more than his share of difficult terrain in his forty-five years of guiding.

As we watched Eduardo and Juan begin the climb to the ram, Francisco said to me, "Not *beeg* sheep." Then he communicated to me in very broken English that I could try for another sheep on his ranch if I so desired. I appreciated the gesture, but I wasn't about to take him up on his surprising offer. Legal considerations aside (and those are rather large considerations), I had just been through perhaps the toughest several days of hunting in my lifetime. I don't think I had another day of hunting left in me.

The guide and I began making our way back to the ridge crest to watch Eduardo, Juan and Beto bring up the ram for a photo session. Swinging his machete, Francisco bushwhacked as I led the burro. Despite my fatigue, I felt deep satisfaction. I had persevered. Despite daunting physical challenges, bone weariness, and earlier disappointment with my missed shot, I now had a Weems sheep to add to my collection of full-mounts in my game room. This adventure would be big smiles and big cigars from here.

Sitting on the ridge in the afternoon sun with Francisco, I glassed for more sheep in a sort of reflex action. If I spotted a great-looking ram, I wasn't about to try for him, even with Francisco's permission. My thoughts turned to the backstraps and coffee we could have when we got back to our spike camp that evening. I assumed we would stay the night at the spike camp and ride out in the morning.

After the rest of our party joined us at the ridge with my prize, I

At last I had my Weems prize and could begin to think about relaxing with a few *cervezas* and a big cigar. But first we would have nearly six hours of rough hiking and riding on our return to our base camp at Francisco's ranch.

posed for a number of photos with the ram's head from different angles. The surrounding terrain made a dramatic backdrop for pictures. From one angle, you could see the intimidating cliffs and pinnacles surrounding us. From another angle, the blue expanse of the gulf rose in the background, calm and hazy in the late afternoon sunlight.

Although sunset was only a couple of hours away, Eduardo announced that we would be returning to base camp that evening rather than sleeping over at the spike camp as I had assumed. My tired body initially rebelled at the five or six hours of rough hiking and riding ahead, but the thought of a snug, comfortable night at

Francisco's ranch was inviting. We left the mountain at about 4:30 in the afternoon descending into an arroyo with a decent trail. Although still steep in places, the ride out was a lot easier than the earlier scramble into these high cliffs where the wild sheep dwelt.

Around 9:30 p.m. we arrived back to where the road had ended and where we had begun riding in four days earlier. A truck met us at the small ranch, and the driver had brought *mucho cervazas.* I had four! (Important to re-hydrate, you know.) We stowed the sheep horns and hide in a corral. Even in the dark, I noticed how tidy and well kept the ranch and outbuildings were. This rugged area was still far from any government services, but these resourceful natives seemed to be making it just fine on their own.

Leaving our mounts behind, our truck pulled into base camp at Francisco's ranch around 10:30 that evening. It was a comforting sight, and the generator in the background made a welcome humming sound. It was late, but certainly not too late for a great dinner already prepared by the women at the ranch.

Enjoying an after-dinner cigar, I stayed up talking with Eduardo despite our fatigue. We went over some of the events of this drama-filled hunt. My outfitter told me that he and the others had been concerned about my having to rappel so much up and down the cliffs. Even though I had surprised them with my grit and conditioning, they had continued to worry. Some of those cliffs going up were a hundred feet or more, he said.

Even before I missed my shot at that first ram, Eduardo and Francisco had already determined not to take me deeper into that dangerous terrain. Beto's spotting the second ram back toward our second spike camp had been fortunate, as the decision had already been made to return to this area. I was just unaware of it at the time. The cliffs going directly down to the spike camp were shorter and less dangerous than those we had climbed positioning for the first sheep.

I found this interesting to hear from Eduardo. Sometimes a hunter is unaware of what an outfitter or guide might be thinking on a hunt like this. It was reassuring to know that Eduardo and the others had been thinking ahead to ensure my safety. Their keeping me in the dark concerning their plans was an innocent attempt to spare me the feeling of being coddled. They really didn't need to worry about that. Rappelling those cliffs in that brutal terrain left me with no feelings of being pampered.

Eduardo also discussed the possibility of another sheep hunt with me in the future. Just hours earlier I had told myself that my wild sheep hunting days were about over. But now, puffing on a cigar in the comfort and security of base camp...I was having second thoughts. Maybe I had another couple of these challenges left in me.

I climbed into my tent that evening with the luxury of a cot to sleep on. The horse blankets I had slept on before were still back with our stock at the end of the roadway, so Francisco gave me the new bedding to ensure my getting a good night's sleep. In my exhausted state, he needn't have worried.

I got up about 6:30 for a breakfast of fried eggs, refried beans, and great coffee with a little sugar. They make their own sugar in these

After the rigors of the challenging Sierra de la Giganta range, I enjoyed several days of rest and recuperation among the families of my outfitter and my guide. This family atmosphere made my hunt on the Baja peninsula special.

parts. It's not refined like that most of us *gringos* are used to.

I luxuriated in the steaming comfort of a "shower" after breakfast. One of the women heated two five-gallon buckets of water and handed me a sixteen-ounce cup. I stood in a shower area and poured the hot water over me. Felt wonderful.

Stretching my aching legs while walking around camp that morning left me again questioning whether I truly had more of these challenging sheep hunts left in me. I still needed a bighorn to complete my third Grand Slam of North American wild sheep. It would need to be a Rocky Mountain bighorn in British Columbia or Alberta.

I watched my ram being caped and salted by my guide and the wranglers. The women in camp were boiling the sheep ribs with vegetables in a large vat. The boiled ribs would be roasted before serving.

Lounging around that morning as the temperature climbed, I drank more coffee and lit a cigar. Eduardo and I had a good discussion about our respective governments. I learned nothing startling from the outfitter, but it was an interesting conversation about two nations with a common border but differing styles of governance.

Late in the afternoon Eduardo drove me to Loreto, where I checked into the Santa Fe Hotel Loreto, a pleasant seaside lodging. After dinner at a nearby restaurant, I collapsed in bed for another night of sound sleep.

The next couple of days were spent exploring Loreto and visiting some of Eduardo's family in the area. We drove through several government checkpoints where we were searched and questioned. The officials' attempts to interdict illegal drugs never end.

The day before I left Loreto, Bo Morgan's son, Nick, invited me to go fishing with him out in the gulf. We hired out a small fishing boat and spent most of the day in this picturesque setting at sea. I even got to experience some turbulence on these usually placid waters.

Before I left Loreto, Bo offered me a "leftover tag" for another sheep hunt in the area that would expire in April. That was only a couple of months away. Before giving an answer, I would first need to get back to Oklahoma and see how my business was going. A few days earlier, I had mostly decided that my desert sheep hunting days were over. Off the mountain and starting to recover, I began to rethink that decision.

I do so enjoy the hunt.

CHAPTER 5

Hunting in the Shadow
Of Volcanoes

(2019)

I declined a leftover sheep tag from Bo Morgan in early 2018, but by 2019 more outdoor adventure on the Baja peninsula beckoned. I accepted a different offer from Bo for a sheep hunt—this time for a *cremnobates* subspecies, less formally known as a Peninsular bighorn. This quest would take me to the rocky, desert terrain around Las Tres Vírgenes volcano complex in northern Baja California Sur.

Mostly recovered from the battering my body took in the Sierra de la Giganta range the previous year, I decided I had at least one more wild sheep hunt left in me. This had become a pattern for me the past several years of sheep hunting: Despairing of future hunts while in the midst of one of these brutal, physical challenges, then booking another of these adventures once my body recovered. I reckoned the end of these extreme outings was getting close—but not just yet.

Thirteen months after the previous year's Weems sheep hunt on the Baja peninsula, I made the same journey from Oklahoma City to Los Angeles and then on to Loreto for another rendezvous with outfitter Eduardo Canett. After my arrival at the airport in Loreto the afternoon of Sunday, March 17, the Mexican officials did their usual thorough inspection of my paperwork, firearm and ammunition. This included photographing my ammunition and the serial

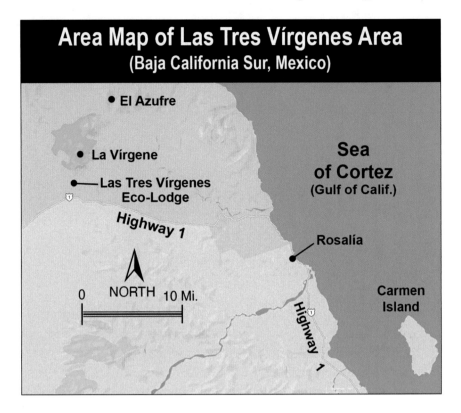

Area Map of Las Tres Vírgenes Area
(Baja California Sur, Mexico)

El Azufre

La Vírgene

Las Tres Vírgenes
Eco-Lodge

Highway 1

Sea
of Cortez
(Gulf of Calif.)

Rosalía

0   NORTH   10 Mi.

Carmen
Island

Highway 1

number on my rifle.

Eduardo arrived as I was going through inspection. We left the airport for the three-hour drive north on Mexico Highway 1 to our base camp on the north end of the state about 20 miles inland from the Gulf of California. On the drive Eduardo told me this sheep hunt would be different from the Weems hunt in 2018. Instead of back-packing, we would be glassing from a boat just offshore the rugged coastline north of the mining town of Santa Rosalía. As the days get hotter in spring, my outfitter explained, the sheep begin migrating toward the cooler temperatures along the coast.

HEARING ABOUT HUNTING from a boat, I flashed back to my first successful desert sheep hunt along the Rio Grande in Big Bend country. There we had glassed the cliffsides abutting the river from my outfitter's flatboat. This hunt with Eduardo would not be while trolling on a slow-moving, shallow river like the Rio Grande. We would be glassing from the exotic and scenic Sea of Cortez, then hiking to the rams once they were located.

My pulse began to quicken. If successful, this Peninsular bighorn hunt would also complete my personal "grand slam" of the four generally accepted subspecies of desert bighorn sheep. As Eduardo continued to brief me on our hunting plans, I thought how fortunate I was to have another hunting adventure like this. I was getting thoroughly pumped.

Late in the day we arrived at our base camp, which was actually the five rustic cabins at Eco Tour Las Tres Vírgenes lodging. The eco-lodge is about fifteen miles west of the coastal town of Santa Rosalía and just north of Hwy. 1. The desert landscape spreading north of the lodge leads to Las Tres Vírgenes (The Three Virgins) complex of three conical-shaped volcanos, part of a volcanic ridge that extends from the northern end of the Baja peninsula toward the center of the Sea of Cortez.

At base camp I reunited with several of the team from my hunt the year before. The 60-something veteran Francisco would help Eduardo guide the hunt, while Alfredo, Armando and a new wrangler

The rustic cabins at Eco Tour Las Tres Vírgenes lodging would serve as our base camp as we hunted for a Peninsular bighorn ram. The camp was situated in a desert landscape with three dormant volcanoes dominating the northern horizon.

113

would glass and provide support. The large team was needed to put a lot of eyes on the large expanse of coastline we would be glassing. Several women at the eco-lodge prepared the meals, and Mexican-style chicken, avocado, and refried beans made for a delightful dinner that evening.

I organized and checked my gear before going to bed. Hoped to take a hot shower before turning in, but someone had failed to turn on the propane water heater. I passed on the cold shower.

I was up at 5:00 and ready for that postponed shower. Still no hot water; still no shower. A last-minute gear check revealed that my video-camera was malfunctioning. If Eduardo couldn't help me get it working, I would have to settle for a lot of still photos on this hunt. (It would mostly be still photos, as it turned out.)

Only coffee and rolls were served for breakfast as we were leaving base camp in a hurry. Just had time to adjust my rifle in the vast desert just behind the eco-lodge. My first shot was off about three inches, but the second was at 9 o'clock inside the bull's-eye. The three dormant volcanos loomed to the north of our camp, eye-popping scenery at sunrise and a memorable landmark for the infrequent tourists and hunters who make the trek to this remote section of the Baja peninsula.

We assembled our party for the short drive to Santa Rosalía, where we would board a 16-foot, open-water fishing boat. Leaving the eco-lodge, Eduardo told me that wild sheep inhabited the

Visitors to the eco-lodge could climb a wooden stairway to the top of a cinder-block tower for a panoramic view of the desert and volcanoes to the north.

The dining hall at the eco-lodge provided delicious meals prepared by several women workers.

slopes of the nearby volcanos, but he believed our chances of finding sheep were better along the coastline where we were headed. Driving eastward to the coast, I looked back with some regret at the diminishing slopes of those mysterious volcanos, imagining a hunt for a prize ram in that striking terrain.

Waiting for our boat to arrive at the harbor in Santa Rosalía, I found a street vendor selling a hearty broth of beef, cilantro and onion. After this late breakfast, I lit up a cigar and watched the locals beginning their week on this Monday morning. Workers swept the streets, and the shops looked neat and tidy. Santa Rosalía was primarily a copper-mining town with three shifts of workers operating continuously.

I didn't get to see much of the town, but I learned that a big part of the local architecture had a strong French influence. A Mexican rancher had discovered copper ore in the area in 1868, and the House of Rothschild in France soon began financing a major mining operation. French businessmen formed the Compagnie Boleo (El Bolo

Copper Company), and by the early 1900s Santa Rosalía had become one of the world's major copper-producing regions. The mines mostly played out by the 1930s, but over the last decade the area has seen a surge of new activity from the reorganized Baja Mining Corporation.

Our party of six boarded the 16-footer piloted by a member of a local family of fishermen, and we made our way along the rocky, broken coastline north of Santa Rosalía. The calm waters of the gulf glistened in the morning sun. Eduardo said we had a three-hour boat ride to our spike camp, but we would stop intermittently to glass for sheep. About thirty minutes outside the harbor, we anchored on a small volcanic rock and began glassing the looming cliffsides along the shoreline.

Strategy for hunting the coastline included all hands glassing the slopes and ridges above us until a ram with good potential was spotted. Our party would then disembark and begin a stalk while maintaining shortwave radio contact with our boat pilot, who would keep a spotting scope on our quarry.

Sounded simple enough, but the brutal climb up the cliffs and through the immense rocks would prove challenging—to put it

A 16-foot fishing boat and a number of pelicans awaited our arrival at the coastal mining town of Santa Rosalía.

politely. Plainly speaking, the terrain in this coastal area is unbelievably nasty. With hardly any beach between land and water, sharp rocks climb steeply upward from the sea to even steeper cliffsides and sharper rocks. Farmers can't make a living in this inhospitable terrain; seems only wild sheep, scorpions and snakes inhabit this rocky desert coastline.

Except for the wiry veteran Francisco and me, most of our party were fit specimens in their thirties and forties. For several years I had been resigned to being one of the oldest members of these hunting parties and tried to compensate by diligent training. I did some special training for this sheep hunt, working with a trainer to better condition my lower body for climbing slopes. I also began lap swimming several times each week, providing a full-body workout. This conditioning paid off in this testy terrain, but the climbing would still take a toll.

Seeing no sheep on our first stop, we cast off and motored northward another 45 minutes or so. We anchored near an area where a few days earlier Eduardo had spotted a group of sheep with a good ram. If not frightened or threatened, sheep will often linger in an area for weeks. Sure enough, these sheep had stayed put.

Although quite scenic, the coastal area around Santa Rosalía is harsh terrain with little to offer beyond a sanctuary for wild sheep, scorpions and snakes.

An *arroyo* (canyon), as shown above, occasionally broke the usually wall-like coastline. These inlets provided a less strenuous access point to explore the hillsides and ridges inland from the coast.

They were a long way off, and the terrain was the usual steep and rocky landscape. But one of the rams looked promising. It was around 11:30. We elected to eat a quick lunch and pursue this ram.

After about an hour of climbing and hiking, we took a break and radioed the boat pilot to get a confirmation on the sheep. The pilot could still see the ram, who was bedded under a tree with two ewes. He would try to get a better assessment of the ram with the spotting scope. With the way ahead steep and rocky, we tarried while waiting for the pilot's appraisal of the ram. It was good we waited. On further review, the pilot judged the ram too young to shoot.

Eduardo advised we check out another promising area nearby while ashore. We hiked and climbed farther inland to the edge of an arroyo, then began a difficult descent in loose gravel toward the bottom of this canyon. Hiking down is usually easier than hiking up, but this steep scramble to the bottom entailed a lot of crawling on hands and knees, and crabbing on our backsides. While maneuvering on my butt down one steep, rocky slide, Eduardo suddenly shouted for my attention.

"Leonardo! Look out!" the outfitter warned. "There *ees* a scorpion behind you."

Still sliding on my backside, I looked back and saw the evil-looking arachnid moving toward me. He appeared to be following me! This was tough country, indeed. Before I began evasive action, the scorpion diverted into some rocks. Relieved, I tried to get a souvenir photo of my erstwhile tormentor but couldn't get a good view of him in the rocks.

The scary critter was one of some sixty species of scorpions found on the Baja peninsula. Dwelling mainly among the rocks on the peninsula, these carnivorous arachnids make a living off the variety of desert insects. Some species of these scorpions produce a venom that can be extremely painful and sometimes fatal. I don't know if the scorpion briefly stalking me was one of the more painful varieties, and I'm glad I didn't find out.

Once we reached the bottom of the arroyo, the hiking got easier. The canyon floor was our expressway back to the coastline, but we still had some glassing to do before returning to set up camp. Mid-afternoon, Eduardo and two others spread out and climbed up the sides of the canyon to look for sheep. Armando and I found a nice place to rest while we waited to hear the results of the search.

With no sheep spotted in the area, the team reassembled in the canyon floor about 5:30 and began hiking back to the coastline. The route was mostly on a downhill grade, but rocky. We probably walked close to twenty miles that day by the time we returned to our earlier beach landing. It was dark by then, and the boat wasn't there.

We turned on a signal light, and soon lights from the boat announced its approach. Our pilot had picked up a couple of hunters and guides, from where I never found out. We boarded for the short ride to a nearby fishing camp where we would spend the night. With eleven now aboard with an assortment of gear, it was pretty crowded.

The pilot assured us the fishing camp wasn't far, no more than a half mile, but it would prove difficult to locate in the dark. The landmark for the camp was an arroyo with a freshwater outlet to the gulf—but try finding that in the dark. We cruised back and forth along the shoreline trying to spot the camp. Shallow reefs forced us to keep our distance from the beach. If the boat propeller hit one of those rocky reefs, we would really have a problem.

Finally, the pilot spotted the fishing camp with the help of a full moon. We pushed toward shore to unload and set up camp. Everyone began to relax, and I took a moment to soak in the surroundings as we neared the beach. Moonlight sparkled across the gulf waters, and dark, rocky cliffs loomed inland up and down the empty coastline. A beautiful setting for a beach campsite.

But in contrast to this pristine natural setting, the fishing camp included a slapdash, open-air shed surrounded by crude wooden railings for drying fish. Pieces of decaying ropes dangled from the railings, remnants of past fishing parties. Years of discarded fish bones of various sizes cluttered the beach. The camp was somewhat of an eyesore in an otherwise unspoiled coastal setting.

We unloaded the boat, set up tents, and sat down to a dinner of coffee and burritos. I had eaten earlier while sitting in the canyon, so I passed on dinner. I turned in at 9:30 and slept comfortably on my air mattress, buffered from the unavoidable rocks and fish bones that covered the beach.

The camp came alive around 5:30. I drank coffee with mocha

The first night out we made our spike camp at a ramshackle fishing camp along the rocky coast. The well-used camp offered a clutter of fish bones on the beach.

chocolate, but passed on the breakfast. I still wasn't too hungry. I've learned to eat just enough to give me energy on these hunts. After the twenty miles of hiking the day before, I decided to put on my compression long johns in preparation for more mileage. These comfortable compression pants seemed to help my legs, providing a little extra support and keeping blood from building up in my lower extremities.

We boarded the crowded boat and cruised the coastline for another look at the sheep seen the day before. Nothing new in the herd, however, just the young ram we had already passed on. We motored another two hours up the coast glassing along the way. No sheep. We pulled into a beach landing to drop off a couple of spotters. They would climb up the high cliffs and glass the rocky slopes unviewable from the boat. Meanwhile, we would cruise a little farther up the coast to glass a new area.

A group of us disembarked at the inlet to an arroyo, and we began trekking up the canyon floor. The bottom of the canyon had its share of rocks, but the uphill grade was not nearly as steep as a direct ascent up the ever-present rocky cliffs abutting the shoreline.

Climbing the high cliffs just off the coast and glassing the rocky slopes inland for sheep became our daily routine on this strenuous coastline hunt.

Alfredo and another spotter went ahead, each climbing up a side of the arroyo to get views unavailable to us from the floor.

If either of the spotters above us saw rams, they were to radio and we would pursue. Most of the hunting party was equipped with one of these short-range radios. We agreed to keep hiking up the arroyo until noon. If no sheep were seen by then, we would turn back toward the beach.

As the hours and difficult miles passed that morning, it became clear that this was turning into another rigorous sheep hunt. Once ashore, we had only our legs to carry us. The terrain was too steep and rocky for horses or mules.

Later that morning Alfredo and the other spotter rejoined us on the canyon floor. "No *beeg* sheep, Leonardo," Alfredo said using his limited English to confirm what I already expected to hear.

We returned down the canyon along the same route we had ascended. It was a rocky hike back to the beach but mostly on a downhill grade. At the shoreline, Eduardo said we would wait for the boat at the beach and relocate to another area. The sea was calm, and the sparkling, clear water provided a view to a depth of twenty feet or more. Finding some shade beside a rocky cliff on the beach, I was struck by how much cooler it was out of the sun. Solar heat gain directly from the rays of Baja sunlight can be brutal.

Our boat arrived around noon, and we proceeded down the coast to pick up the two spotters we had dropped off that morning by the high cliffs. Arriving at the cliffs, we were in for some drama. Attempting a descent down a wide crevice in the steep rock face, the two spotters had become stranded about halfway down. The pitch became too vertical to continue descending and too difficult to go back up. Eduardo climbed up close to the stranded spotters and was able to talk them down safely. I think the pair had lost their nerve and needed some moral support.

When they all got down to the beach, they were laughing—but it seemed a nervous laugh to me. It was a long drop from where they had been stranded, and the risk of serious injury or death was real. My outfitter Eduardo certainly earned his pay that day.

We motored down the coastline a short way and again dropped off the two spotters at an inlet to another arroyo. Continuing on, the

Our party often split up and communicated by short-wave radio in our futile efforts to find sheep in the rugged coastal terrain.

boat dropped off me, Eduardo and Francisco at another inlet to an area the outfitter had not hunted in several years. After an hour of difficult hiking and climbing up the canyon, we began glassing the sides of a sizable mountain. Still no sheep.

Moving farther up the canyon for another hour or so, the climbing and scrambling began to take a toll on me. Eduardo suggested I find a place to rest, while he and Francisco pushed ahead. They would radio me if they spotted a good ram. Sounded like a good plan to me and my drained legs.

The temperature was around 85 degrees as I waited in my rest area. I thought how the sheep would be bedded down in shade somewhere. They would be difficult to spot until they started moving again in the late afternoon. And as Eduardo had reminded me earlier, the Baja is desert country with only small populations of wild sheep. You can't find what's not there.

An hour later, my outfitter and guide returned from their futile search. Eduardo told Francisco and me to stay put while he took a quick look at another area. It was getting late enough in the day that the sheep would be getting up to feed. But he returned in less than an hour without good news. We began the two-hour march back to the sea.

Approaching the beach as the sun began to lower, I was glad to see the shining surf lapping the shoreline. It had been another exhausting day of rock hopping and climbing. I slumped into the boat, and we picked up the rest of our crew along the way down the coastline to a new spike camp.

After a beef stew dinner, I had coffee with mocha and a cigar. Hoping to reassure me, Eduardo said we would glass one more area in the morning. If no good rams were spotted, we would cruise back to Santa Rosalía and regroup that evening at the eco-lodge. From there, we could ride and hike out to look for sheep on the slopes of the volcanoes north of base camp.

Crawling into my tent that evening, I was glad to hear Eduardo had a feasible backup plan. Poor outfitters don't plan to fail; they just don't plan. We had a plan. I was going to sleep well.

This kind of exhausting rock hopping was typical of some of the arduous climbs off the beach and onto the higher ground inland.

At least I thought I was going to sleep well. The wind turned ferocious during the night. It even drowned out Eduardo's loud snoring in the tent beside me. My tent shook like crazy and finally collapsed. I repeatedly got up to reset my tent after it kept cratering in the gale. Eduardo's tent had collapsed on him, but his continued snoring told me he was oblivious to it all. It was a long night for me.

I got dressed in my tent at 5:00, and by then the wind had died down. Our equipment was scattered all over camp. But the eggs and tortillas for breakfast picked up my spirit.

We packed up and headed out in the boat just after dawn. We dropped off a spotter several miles down the shoreline then proceeded down the coast to another inlet. I disembarked with Eduardo, Francisco and Armando, and we began hiking up the canyon.

After a difficult, rocky climb inland, we soon came to a nearly vertical rocky slope. Already slowing, it was obvious I was going to have trouble. Eduardo suggested I hover while the rest of the party split up to search the nearby area for sheep. If any of them saw a good ram, he would return to guide me on a stalk. If no sheep were seen, we would regroup around 10:30 or 11 at my location and make our way back to the boat.

Our bad luck continued. The glassers spotted only ewes and immature rams. We started our trek back to the boat but had a difficult climb down the rocky slope that had so taxed me earlier that morning. Fortunately, it wasn't too far through the toughest part. By noon, we were back at the boat.

After picking up the spotter dropped off earlier, we began the boat ride back to Santa Rosalía. The sea was still choppy from the winds during the night. The boat bounced on the water making for a rough ride. I could really feel it in my back—and it didn't feel good. Once again I was reminded that my extreme outdoor adventures couldn't go on forever.

We left the boat at the harbor in late morning and began the 45-minute drive back to the eco-lodge. This was Day 3 of the sheep hunt, and I was yet to chamber a round. Hunting the rocky coastline had proved fruitless and disappointing, even if quite the adventure. But I was encouraged by Eduardo's taking the initiative to try a new strategy. I would get a chance to hunt the slopes of those exotic volcanos after all.

As we exited north from Hwy. 1 toward the eco-lodge. I got a grand view of our new hunting range, Las Tres Vírgenes volcano complex. The lodge perches on a short hill about two miles north of the highway, providing a stunning view of the three dormant volcanos several miles farther to the north.

With the three volcanos aligned from northeast to southwest, El Viejo, is the oldest of the three and the farthest from the lodge. El Azufre sits in the middle, and the youngest, El Vírgen, lies to the southwest of its sister volcanos. At 6,400 feet above sea level at its summit, El Vírgen is the most conspicuous of the trio. Owing to its prominence, this single dormant volcano is often called Las Tres Vírgenes—although that actually refers to the complex of all three volcanoes. These are the only stratovolcanoes (conical volcanoes) on the Baja peninsula.

Several miles of relatively flat, thornscrub desert lay between the lodge and Las Tres Vírgenes. This arid expanse is covered with a variety of cactus and desert flora not unlike the area I had hunted the year before west of Loreto. Climbing up the wooden staircase of the lodge's stone lookout tower provided a stunning vista of the miles of desert preceding the volcanos to the north. Truly an impressive setting for a desert sheep hunt. I felt a restored spring in my drained legs.

When we arrived at the lodge, several new hunters and Nick Morgan, Bo's son, were in the dining room. We all sat down to a meal in a kind of meet-and-greet session, which I generally find tiresome. I had to listen to a number of banal hunting stories while sitting down to an otherwise well-prepared lunch.

With a lot of daylight still left, Eduardo told me to get ready for a drive out to the edge of the volcano range for some glassing. I was happy to get back to my room with a bathroom and bed, even though I had little time to enjoy the luxury. On the walk to my cabin, I saw several people gathered around the sidewalk to my quarters. The owner of the lodge had cornered a rattlesnake, which he seemed to have no fear of. I took a photo of him gripping the deadly snake near its head as he displayed it.

The Baja California rattlesnake is a medium-sized pit viper native to the coast and islands of northwest Mexico. Like other pit vipers, it is venomous. Strangely, at least to me, it's a protected species of the Mexican government. While I would have been happy to dispatch the evil-looking critter with my rifle, the lodge owner carried him away from the cabins and released him. *Good riddance and stay gone*, I thought.

By early afternoon I was riding through the desert in Eduardo's pickup toward the volcanos. The roadway was likely constructed to accommodate traffic to the geothermal electric generation plant west of El Azufre, the center volcano in the complex. Eduardo dropped me off with a spotter, while he and another spotter drove off to glass a different area. We would be glassing in the shadow of El Vírgen, the most impressive of the trio of volcanoes.

As soon as I got situated, I realized I didn't have my binoculars or my rangefinder with me. Eduardo and I had identical Eberlestock

packs, and I had grabbed his by mistake when exiting the truck. I could do little but enjoy the scenery and wait for my outfitter to pick me up later in the afternoon.

None of us located a good ram that afternoon, but I did get a good look of where I would now be hunting desert sheep. The stately

Puzzling to gringos like me, the venomous Baja California rattlesnake is a protected species of the Mexican government.

127

saguaros and other exotic desert growth looked familiar, but the conical volcanos dominating the skyline were a novelty. They certainly added some color to this hunt. Now, if we could only find a ram worth shooting.

We returned to the lodge, our base camp, in late afternoon. Several new faces were now at the eco-lodge. The winner of a drawing at the annual Sheep Show, a hunter from Seattle had brought along a friend to enjoy the experience. An outfitter from British Columbia also joined us that evening in the dining hall. Eduardo and I discussed plans to return to the volcanoes in the morning.

Someone had finally remembered to turn the propane water heater on. I luxuriated in a hot shower before crawling into my comfortable bed. The shower was my first since I had left my hotel room in Los Angeles—three days earlier and prior to a lot of sweaty hiking along the Baja coastline.

JUST ANOTHER THURSDAY MORNING in the working world, March 21 dawned cool and bright on the Baja peninsula. I was up well before daylight. Eduardo had told me the evening before that we had close to a seven-hour trek to the slopes of El Azufre, the center volcano and the most likely area to find a good ram. Unless we got lucky the first day out, we would stay overnight in a spike camp near El Vírgene. I packed for several more days in the field.

The previous three days of rock climbing and the bumpy boat ride back to Santa Rosalía had left me with battered, drained legs and a painfully sore back. To aid me on the long hike ahead that day, Eduardo planned to put me on a burro the first few miles. This would get me across the relatively flat expanse of desert preceding the rocky slopes and ridges that marked volcano country.

After a quick breakfast of rolls and coffee, we left the eco-lodge and headed toward the sun-beaten slopes of Las Tres Vírgenes. We drove in Eduardo's truck for a couple of miles until we left the roadway. I then mounted the female burro, or jenny, provided by my outfitter. She had an agreeable personality, but unfortunately her saddle didn't.

The ride across the desert was reminiscent of previous desert sheep hunts dodging through a tangle of cactus and thornscrub. The terrain had the usual variety of cacti: saguaro, organ pipe, barrel, cholla and prickly pear. Towering over the other varieties of cactus, the different configurations of saguaro were as mesmerizing as usual. With their human-like projections of limbs, it's so easy to personify this desert royalty. Noting these different sizes and shapes of saguaro broke the monotony of the first few miles.

After riding about an hour, I decided hiking with a bad back would be easier than riding a donkey with an ill-fitting saddle and stirrups. I left my jenny at our spike camp, where we would return for the night if the hunt was not concluded.

The desert gave way to the rocky lower slopes of the volcano complex, and the climbing began as we ascended the steep, rock-strewn passages. This climbing may not have been as torturous as the coastal ascents of the previous three days, but the route was plenty steep.

We skirted the eastern slopes of El Vírgen, the dominant sister of the three volcanos. The morning sunlight brilliantly displayed her

I had hoped to ease my aching legs by riding on this jenny, but unfortunately for me the saddle and stirrups didn't fit. Accompanying our party as an observer was a Wyoming outdoorsman named Leon, pictured above.

slopes. The higher slopes leading to the crater at the summit were nearly vertical, giving an appearance more like the peak of a mountain. Rising 5,300 feet from the desert floor and with a summit more than 6,000 feet above sea level, the big sister certainly qualified for mountain status. Although a Jesuit missionary reported an eruption of El Vírgen in 1746, this could have been no more than a venting of hot gases. Radiometric dating of charcoal fragments in the complex put the most recent eruption around 3,500 B.C.

We hiked, scrambled and climbed for about an hour as we approached the slopes of El Azufre, the center volcano north of big sister, El Vírgene. This was hard going. I stopped for a moment to look back at the distant desert floor now below us. A dozen miles or so on the eastern horizon, the gulf waters glistened. With Las Tres Vírgenes volcanic complex the most scenic attraction in this region, I considered it a bonus to be sheep hunting on these slopes.

By mid-morning we were on the rocky southern slopes of El Azufre and starting to glass sheep above us. Several appeared to be mature rams. We had to skirt the side of a high ridge to get above them. After a testy scramble, we ranged the rams at a little more than 1,000 yards. Two looked like real shooters, and I felt a familiar tingle of excitement. But we would have a difficult time getting into position near these rams.

After the climb from hell, we maneuvered within a couple of hundred yards of our quarry—at least that's what Eduardo told me. I couldn't see the sheep! The rams are about the same color of the rocks in this area, and I wasn't used to hunting these slopes. My eyes just couldn't distinguish between the rocks and the sheep.

Great! Here I was only a couple of hundred yards from a couple of good rams, and I couldn't find them in this unfamiliar terrain. Eduardo became exasperated, beside himself trying to point them out to me. *"There, Leonardo, there,"* he whispered fiercely pointing in the direction of the rams I couldn't see. After four days of tremendous struggle to get into a position like this, and all I could see was rocks and thornscrub.

I asked my outfitter to range the rams exactly, hoping that might help me pinpoint their location. But by this time they were starting to move higher and away, Eduardo told me. You can rarely get this

The rocks and thornscrub along the hillsides made it difficult for me to see the rams my outfitter had spotted. After he ranged them and told me the distance, I was finally able to discern them along the distant slope.

close to wild sheep without making them nervous, and predictably they were getting antsy. *And I still couldn't see them!*

Finally, I made out the two rams slowly moving above and away from us. By then, Eduardo ranged them at 400 yards. I got into a prone position using Eduardo's pack as a rest. I adjusted the bullet-drop compensator, keeping one eye on the ram in front.

He was still moving higher. I couldn't wait much longer for him to stop. I silently begged him to pause and take that fatal look back at what was making him nervous. But the ram just kept moving away.

No time left. I would have to take a 400-yard shot at this slow-moving target. I put the crosshairs slightly in the front of the ram and followed his movement slowly...slowly...and gently squeezed the trigger. A split-second after I felt the recoil, I thought I heard the bullet hit the rocks just beyond the ram, who quickly disappeared from view. I felt fairly certain I had missed, but Eduardo said I had hit him. Had the bullet gone through the ram before hitting the rock? I didn't think so. As much as I hoped to have mortally wounded the ram, I was skeptical of Eduardo's assessment.

As we waited for the ram to come back into view, Eduardo suddenly pointed in another direction below us: *"Leonardo! Look down there!"* This time I had no trouble seeing what he was pointing at—two more good-looking rams on a steep slope at about 200 yards. Inexplicably, they had not taken off when I fired. After several days of frustration, I suddenly had multiple opportunities for a ram. I couldn't believe it!

I felt certain I had missed that ram earlier, so I was ready to pivot to the new target. The new ram I zeroed in on looked really good. I was ready to shoot, but Eduardo firmly refused permission. We first needed to investigate the results of my earlier shot, he insisted. Had I wounded the ram or missed him entirely?

As certain as I felt that I had cleanly missed the shot and as ready as I now was to shoot the handsome ram just below me, I knew my outfitter was right. As hard as it would be to wait for Francisco's investigation of the earlier target area, I would have to be patient. If the guide found no dead or wounded ram, or no blood, I had the green light to target one of the rams below us.

The wait was excruciating. I watched Francisco climb the nasty, rocky slope toward where we had last seen the ram I shot at. I also kept an eye on the two rams below us, who seemed strangely unperturbed by our presence. The minutes ticked by. I could hardly keep my finger off the trigger as I eyed the two rams below through my rifle scope. "Wait, Leonardo," Eduardo kept saying in a low voice, worried that I wouldn't be able to restrain myself.

My outfitter was rightly concerned about my faltering self-restraint. Fifteen, then twenty minutes passed, and Francisco had not come back into view. He was searching diligently for the results of my rifle shot, and obviously not finding anything. Even a trace of fresh blood would have prompted him to radio us. My hopes rose with each passing minute. The guide was finding no evidence that I had hit the ram. But how much longer would the two rams below stay put?

One of the rams finally stood and looked in our direction. I got a good view of him at 200 yards. I told Eduardo that I would shoot him if Francisco ever gave us the words we wanted to hear. My outfitter continued to scrutinize the two rams through his binoculars. He told me to take another close look at the ram still bedded. This calmer ram looked even better to my outfitter. I wasn't sure.

Where was Francisco? Why hadn't we heard from him? These two rams below weren't going to linger forever, especially with one of them standing and looking nervous. Eduardo kept cautioning me to wait. With the tension already unbearable, the second ram stood up. Now we had two nervous rams below us. Where was Francisco?

Finally, about thirty minutes after he had left us, Francisco radioed...no downed ram, no trace of blood. Apparently, a clean miss on my part. I was good to go. As it turned out, it was better that I had been forced to wait—the second ram to stand did appear better than the first one, just as Eduardo had assessed. Both of these desert bighorns were now slowly moving away from us. But all of my attention was focused solely on the second ram, and I was cleared for the shot—finally.

Yes, the second ram looked magnificent. At about 250 yards, he stopped, turned, and looked in our direction. One problem—he was directly facing us. His profile was as narrow as it could get. The target area on his chest was about six-inches wide.

Eduardo advised me to wait until he turned broadside. But after thirty minutes of tension, I didn't feel like waiting. I had practiced enough that I knew I could make this shot. I put that earlier missed shot out of my mind as I concentrated on that six-inch area on this big ram's chest. I knew Eduardo preferred I wait...but my waiting was over.

I took the shot. Bingo! The ram dropped where he stood. He wasn't going anywhere. I was shouting. Eduardo was shouting. I heard Francisco shouting in the distance. After four days, this was the moment!

I felt a combination of relief and elation. This had been a trying half hour. First the missed shot, then the unbelievable good fortune of two good rams still within range, then the interminable wait to hear from Francisco. Then Eduardo telling me to wait for the ram to turn broadside—and my taking the lower-percentage shot anyway. Wow! What a series of exciting, nerve-wracking moments.

The more I studied the downed ram with my binoculars, the more impressed I was. Even on the ground, this guy looked big. I couldn't wait to see him up close.

But seeing him up close wasn't going to be easy, even though he was only 250 yards from us. The steeply sloped, rocky sides of El Azufre didn't make for beeline hiking. We would have a long, circuitous scramble to get to this ram.

The rocky, cliffy, steep terrain was every bit the physical torture I thought it would be. It took about an hour for us to get to the ram, who was lying on his side on a steep, narrow ledge. Seeing this downed ram up close, I could hardly have been more pleased. He appeared around seven years old, fully mature but not old. Eduardo said the bases on the horns were at least sixteen inches. The fully curled horns had some typical brooming on the tips.

This *cremnobates* ram completed my personal slam of the four desert bighorn sheep. And he appeared to be the largest of any of my previous desert prizes. Everyone in our party was thrilled with my success. We spent about an hour celebrating and taking

This Peninsular bighorn sheep (*Ovis canadensis cremnobates*) would be the largest of my desert bighorn prizes. Harvesting this bighorn was made all the more memorable by the exotic volcanic landscape where we had found him.

pictures with the ram. The narrow ledge where he had fallen made for some difficult maneuvering while posing for the camera. Leon, a personable outdoorsman from Wyoming about my age, had joined our hunting party that morning and posed with me and my ram.

It was a little past noon when we began discussing our return, hoping to make it to Eduardo's truck before dark. My outfitter told Leon and me to go ahead while the team finished quartering and caping my ram. We started down a steep rocky slide through a boulder field to the saddle where we had dropped our packs earlier. At the saddle one of Eduardo's wranglers was already waiting with a couple of burros to help pack out the meat and hide.

Leon and I picked our way as best we could through the jumble of rocks, cactus and gravel slides for a couple of hours before arriving at the spike camp where I had left the jenny with the ill-fitting saddle. Drained from four days of rock climbing and hiking, my tired legs were starting to fail me. I decided to endure the uncomfortable

My elation at taking this bighorn prize soon faded as we all considered the long, difficult route back to our truck far below. The truck could be seen shimmering in the distance miles away, but getting back would be a challenge.

saddle on the jenny to get to the truck, which we could occasionally see glimmering in the far distance below but still several hours away in this terrible terrain.

But the jenny had not gotten to know me too well from our short ride earlier, and she refused to be saddled by a couple of guys she barely knew. I would have to battle on with nothing left in my legs. We left the burro for the team still coming up behind, who could doubtless use another burro to help pack out the meat, hide and gear. We made it down to another saddle, then heard Alfredo coming up behind us.

Soldiering on, I began to stumble a little from jelly legs, pain in my back, and sheer exhaustion. Leon began pulling ahead. I appreciated Alfredo's company as I gritted my teeth and battled on.

About two miles from the truck, Eduardo and the team caught up with us. They took a couple of packs off the jenny and urged me to climb aboard. All in by then, I didn't have much choice. Aboard the burro, I was at least able to keep up with the team as we closed in on the truck. I don't know which hurt worse—my knees from the ill-fitting tack or my sore back from the previous day's boat ride.

Just before sunset, we made it to the truck. Relief at last—and a cooler full of beer! Renewed, I broke out the cigars. Everyone was celebrating. After a brief rest and a couple of beers, those earlier tortuous miles melted into the past.

We pulled into the base camp at the eco-lodge around 7:30. The cooks at the lodge had prepared a great dinner for us. Fresh meat and vegetables, nothing processed.

Afterward, I meandered down to my cabin, utterly exhausted but smiling inside. What a great ram! What a great day! What a great life!

I showered and hit the bed, not moving a muscle until 7:00 the next morning.

THE NEXT DAY SEEMED TO BE in slow motion, for me and the rest of the base camp. I still had a tag for a black-tailed deer and thought we might go out in the field later in the day. But I think Eduardo and his team needed to recharge their batteries. So did I.

After getting up at 7:00 and reading some from my Bible, I

moseyed down to the dining hall for coffee and hot chocolate. Not much going on. I sat drinking coffee for a while reviewing the momentous events of the day before. I pondered what kept those two rams below us from bolting when I shot at and missed that ram above us. Wild sheep can be unpredictable, and I'm sure glad my new prize ram had been. His unusually calm demeanor proved fatal for him but provided me with a great trophy.

Later in the day Eduardo and Francisco measured and scored my ram's head. I couldn't believe it—at 173-plus, it was a Boone & Crockett head! And the biggest sheep I had ever killed. Another of the hunters came in that afternoon with an even slightly bigger set of horns. So we had two Boone & Crockett ram's heads in our base camp at the same time.

Some of Eduardo's team began leaving, and those remaining were more into celebrating the successful hunts than taking me on a deer hunt. But I could use the day off and was perfectly content helping the cooks butcher the meat with their loud native music playing in the background. We roasted the sheep on a grill and had a great celebratory meal that evening. The party was still underway when I began to fade around 7:30. We were leaving early the next morning on the deer hunt, and I needed another full night's sleep.

We didn't leave the eco-lodge till 7:00 the next morning—a late start for a deer hunt. With the pickup slowly cruising on the desert road north of the lodge, I stood in the bed resting my rifle over the cab. This was similar to the "high-racking" technique used when I had hunted Coues deer in Sonora years earlier. With my head above the cab, I could see over the thornscrub terrain. But our late start likely precluded seeing deer that morning, so before midday we retreated to the eco-lodge for lunch and cigars.

We made another foray later in the afternoon. Coming to the end of the desert road near sunset, we turned around and began a slow drive back toward the lodge. We finally spotted two black-tails, one older with a good rack. Eduardo got excited and urged me to take the shot.

Standing in the back of the pickup, I used my backpack atop the cab as a rifle rest. After some initial trouble finding the buck in my rifle scope, I put my crosshairs on him at around 200 yards. He was slowly walking away with his backside toward us, so I hit him with a "Texas heart shot"—usually quite effective. I took another shot as he disappeared but wasn't sure to what effect.

But neither round immediately dropped my quarry, and we tracked the blood trail until dark. The deer probably had not gone far, but locating him in the moonlight would be difficult. We decided to come back the next morning for the recovery.

The team spread out the next morning looking for blood and tracks. Alfredo said the deer was limping. He based this on his observing a shallow track from one of the deer's rear legs. After about thirty minutes, Eduardo found the deer a couple of hundred yards from where he had been hit. He was dead but still warm. And he was huge, an 11-pointer with a large body for a black-tailed deer. Eduardo said it was probably the largest black-tail any of his clients had taken.

"*Muy grandé* sheep and *muy grandé* deer," I joked with my Mexican team members as we took photos with the deer. After photos,

Noted outfitter Bo Morgan said the 11-point black-tailed deer was the nicest ever taken by any of his clients, and he believed it to be close to a Safari Club International record.

This wrangler threw the large black-tail over his shoulder and carried him away as if he weighed no more than a sack of potatoes. Note the volcanoes of Las Tres Vírgenes in the background.

one of the new wranglers tied him up, put him on his shoulders, and walked out like he was carrying no more than a bag of groceries. I walked behind him and found myself hurrying to keep up. That guy was strong!

A few days later, Nick Morgan sent a picture of my prize to his father, Bo. Bo said he believed the deer would be close to a Safari Club International world record for a black-tail. He also said it was the nicest black-tailed deer ever taken by any of his clients.

After taking my *cremnobates* prize, I had been indifferent about deer hunting and decided I would only shoot one that was impressive. Well, this guy really fit the bill! I left the eco-lodge totally fulfilled from my outdoor adventures. And with my legs starting to recover, I began to think how I just might have another one or two of these extreme desert hunts left in me after all.

I spent the next few days before departure sightseeing in the area. Eduardo drove me down to the small fishing village of Mulegé, where he lived. The town is right on the gulf and not far south of Santa Rosalía. I stayed in a hotel there, and the next day my outfitter drove me to the Santa Fe Hotel Loreto, the seaside lodging where I had stayed the year before. When leaving the next day, I tried to pay the hotel bill with a hundred-dollar bill, but the front desk wouldn't take it. Fear of counterfeiting in Mexico is widespread— and well-justified.

While in Loreto I walked down to the beach to take in the gulf air and scenery. All the locals I encountered were friendly and welcoming. Yet the serenity at the beach was jarred by the sight of a marine patrol riding in an open-bed pickup with a turret-mounted machine gun. I also noted a large presence of municipal police and Federales—who I was informed were largely controlled by the drug- and human-trafficking cartels.

The Baja peninsula is a region of wild and scenic beauty, but in a land with more than its share of domestic problems. Still, the full-mounts of the two desert rams and two deer I took on the peninsula will always remind me of the two wonderful outdoor adventures I enjoyed there.

CHAPTER 6

The Return of the Desert Bighorn

Most who hunt any species of North American bighorn sheep are aware that in 2024 better opportunities for pursuing this game exist than forty or fifty years ago. This also holds true for the four subspecies of North American bighorns that inhabit the desert regions of southwest United States and northwest Mexico.

Good information on the increased quantities of bighorn sheep and the cooperative efforts that brought this about can be found in the impressive 1999 book, *Return of Royalty: Wild Sheep of North America.* Authored by Dale Toweill and Valerius Geist and jointly published by Boone and Crockett Club and Foundation for North American Wild Sheep, this authoritative work still informs efforts by various groups concerned with the future of these wildlife icons. This can also be said of the more recent 2015 book *Desert Bighorn Sheep: Wilderness Icon* by Marc Jorgensen and Jeff Young, with the scope of this work restricted to desert bighorn sheep.

Both of these books are valuable for any assessment of the present state of desert sheep and their future in the U.S. Southwest and northern Mexico. It is fortunate that two such quality sources of information are available for those of us interested in both the hunting and conservation of these desert dwellers. Much of this chapter draws heavily on these two authoritative sources.

North American Desert Sheep Hunting

Decline and Restoration

The populations of wild sheep in the western United States and northern Mexico in the early 1800s has been estimated as high as one million, with a significant portion of this number divided among the four subspecies of desert bighorn. By the early twentieth century, however, desert sheep were nearing extinction. Officials estimate that even today desert sheep populations are only about 5 percent of their numbers from two centuries earlier. The declining numbers of these arid nomads resulted primarily from the same forces that decimated their bighorn cousins in other regions: isolated rangelands cut off from migratory routes, competition with and disease from domestic livestock (especially domestic sheep), and to a lesser extent predation by hunters who targeted wild sheep as a source of food.

The national polices that may have saved the desert sheep from extinction began early in the twentieth century with U.S. President Theodore Roosevelt and Canadian Prime Minister Sir Wilfred Laurier. Their shared vision of public policies for the conservation of North American

Working with Canadian Prime Minister Sir Wilfred Laurier, U.S. President Theodore Roosevelt fostered a scientific approach to wildlife management in North America. In conjunction with this, Roosevelt helped establish a politically effective voice for wildlife with the creation of the Boone and Crockett Club.

wildlife would ultimately save much of the imperiled flora and fauna of their two countries and establish a science-based approach to their conservation goals.

The achievements of these two far-sighted leaders included the setting aside of large tracts of public lands to be conserved for future generations as well as a politically effective voice for wildlife with the creation of the Boone and Crockett Club. The scientific approach, fostered in particular by Roosevelt, gave rise to the profession of wildlife biologists—professionals who established a scientific basis for effective wildlife management.

North American wildlife management largely evolved into a conservation effort with public oversight and legislative debate. The benefits of this approach and concurrent efforts of government officials, wildlife professionals, concerned outdoorsmen, and private

Desert Bighorn Population Estimates by State/Year

State	1960[1]	1993[4]	2018[5]	2024[6]
Arizona	3,000-3,500	6,000	5,000-5,500	6,000
Baja North[2]	2,500	2,500	2,500	2,500
Baja South[3]	350	350	350	350
California	1,800-2,100	4,300-4,325	5,100	5,000
Colorado	0	475	540	600
Nevada	1,500-2,000	5,295	10,300	11,000
N. Mexico	400-500	295	1,200	1,400
Sonora	1,500	1,800	2,000	3,000
Texas	Remnant	400	1,500	1,500
Utah	Remnant	2,200-2,250	2,900	3,000
Total	12,000	23,600	31,600	34,350

[1]McCutchen, H. E., *Desert Bighorn Sheep*, 1995   [2]CA Fish & Game 98(1):51-59, 2012.
[3]CITES & Livelihoods Case Study (2019).   [4]Desert Bighorn Council reports, 1993.
[5]"State Status Reports," Desert Bighorn Council, 2019.
[6]Estimated by author from various states' publications and websites.

landowners have contributed greatly to the near-miraculous restoration of much of the continent's threatened flora and fauna. While much still needs to be done and wildlife conservation efforts will always be ongoing, we should recognize the success achieved in North America in the last seventy-five years.

The return of the desert bighorn and bighorn sheep in general reflects some of the fruits of these larger conservation efforts. (See chart on previous page.) Certainly this work is more obvious with the increased white-tailed deer and elk populations, but the increased numbers of desert bighorn and opportunities for sheep hunters are undeniable. A review of wild sheep conservation efforts over the last century are instructive of how these successes were attained and how they can be continued.

Wildlife biologists working to conserve and expand wild sheep populations have come to recognize three key goals guiding their efforts. The first is to maintain sheep populations in areas they currently inhabit. Obviously, these established herds have already adapted to these hospitable ranges, so working to maintain these animals in their established homelands is axiomatic. Preserving these extant populations may be the low-hanging fruit of wild sheep management.

A second and more challenging goal is reintroducing and expanding sheep populations into areas formerly occupied before their near extinction in the nineteenth century. A corollary to this is the introduction and expansion of herds into now-suitable terrain where sheep might not have thrived in previous periods under different conditions. Establishing these populations where none currently exist, or ever exited, obviously requires careful planning by wildlife officials and cooperation from local stakeholders. While difficult, this goal is still a key to restoring wild sheep populations beyond their recently improved but still tenuous numbers.

A third goal is to maintain a maximum of the evolved genetic diversity within existing herds of wild sheep. Safeguarding this range of biological variance enables these herds to adapt to changing conditions in their environment. This genetic diversity also acts as a sort of brain trust for the overall population in an area—a storehouse for the inhabitants' knowledge of their environment. Evolved genetic diversity occurs naturally, and the introduction of too many new sheep into an established population can weaken the herd's overall understanding of their environment. This lack of understanding can result in a herd's failure to thrive—or even to survive.

While most wildlife officials view these goals as vital to the restoration of North American wild sheep, various management strategies and practices have emerged to reach these goals. For example, and related to the second and third goals above, is the now widespread recognition of the importance of maintaining interconnected mountain corridors for wild sheep migrations. Reducing fencing and providing access over highways are among some of the methods of reducing the isolation and fragmentation of sheep herds.

The varied terrains, legal and social environments, differences among sheep populations, and other factors require a dynamic approach to wildlife conservation. Methods may vary from region to region. What works in Nevada might be impractical in west Texas.

The intricacies and expertise of wildlife management regarding wild sheep are far beyond the scope of this guidebook for sheep hunters. Still, sportsmen who seek these ram trophies are stakeholders in these management efforts. As such, they benefit from a better understanding of wildlife officials' goals and objectives regarding the hunting of these animals. Sheep hunters provide a significant part of the revenues needed to restore and maintain these herds. A reciprocal and mutually beneficial relationship exists between increased opportunities for wild sheep trophy hunters and the conservation of this game.

Most agency officials understand how maximizing the opportunities for hunters to harvest a trophy ram can help fund their efforts to restore and maintain these sheep. Familiar to most outdoor sportsmen, this permitting system usually requires the sheep hunter to focus on a small segment of the mature rams in a population, a segment differentiated by horn size. Outside of providing funds for conservation efforts, carefully managing these types of harvests can actually enhance the overall health of the herd.

With this approach, hunter quotas are closely controlled. The number of hunters allowed is usually increased inversely proportional to the likelihood of success. For example, more hunters are allowed to hunt in areas with extremely difficult terrain (of which I am intimately acquainted).

Hunting regulations for these trophies also targets the older, most knowledgeable rams (and sometimes ewes). Yet if too many of these elder statesmen of the herd are taken, the group's social stability and overall knowledge of habitat can be adversely affected. Officials usually take extreme care to prevent this, primarily through the aforesaid permitting system that allows only a few of these older, trophy rams to be harvested each season.

Besides focusing the harvest on the oldest rams in a population, wildlife officials use several other regulatory measures to lessen adverse effects of hunting wild sheep:

• Limiting the number of rams taken each season to less than 10 percent of the mature males in an identified herd. This ensures that the social well-being of the herd is maintained.

• Allowing harvest of a limited number of adult ewes to keep the ewe/lamb numbers within carrying capacity of the herd. This enhances the survivability and growth rate of these new members of the herd.

Scientific approaches to lessen adverse effects of hunting wild sheep include allowing the harvest of a limited number of adult ewes to keep the ewe/lamb numbers within capacity of the herd.

The conservation and restoration efforts for North American desert sheep have resulted in significantly increased opportunities for both those who appreciate viewing wildlife and for hunters who cherish these iconic trophies.

• Scheduling hunting seasons to keep hunters off the herd's grazing lands during critical periods like the winter months. This prevents sheep from abandoning more favorable ranges during stressful times of the year.

The results of these conservation and restoration efforts on North American desert sheep populations have been dramatic, especially in the last half century, and these increased numbers have varied by state in both the United States and Mexico. Fortunately for all stakeholders, the trend is upward. Viewing these various states' progress is both informative and encouraging to outdoor sportsmen.

Arizona

Numerous reports of a bounty of desert bighorn sheep (mostly *Ovis canadensis mexicana*) were reported in Arizona in the mid-1800s, but their rapid decline precludes accurate estimates of their population prior to widespread settlement in the late 1800s. So dramatic was their decimation that the Arizona Territorial Legislature in 1893 passed a five-year moratorium on the hunting of bighorn sheep. This was well in advance of the conservation efforts led by the Roosevelt administration in the early 1900s.

Even with Arizona officials' early efforts, by the late 1930s only about 1,000 desert bighorns were left in the state, with most of these along the Colorado River. Yet it was noted that scattered herds of desert sheep still survived in some parts of the state, and the near extirpation of these sheep was linked more to the arrival of domestic livestock than poaching. Preservation efforts began in earnest in 1939 with the establishment of the Kofa and Cabeza Prieta game ranges for sheep and other state wildlife.

Studies in the 1950s carefully located what remnant herds still existed in Arizona and the habitat needed to maintain them. Significantly, these studies resulted in the recommendation that the desert sheep be isolated from domestic livestock and feral burros. Perhaps as important, a recommendation was also made for the initiation of regulated hunting of these sheep and reintroduction programs in formerly inhabited desert ranges. A slow but steady increase in desert bighorn sheep grew from these studies and recommendations.

In the decades that followed, more than 1,200 desert bighorns were captured and relocated in historic habitat. The comeback of desert sheep in Arizona has been dramatic. As the twentieth century came to a close, an estimated 6,000 bighorns were living in remote

Black Mtns.

AZ

Kofa Mtns.

Sierra Pintas Growler Mtns.

● Concentrations
Nelsoni   Mexicana

areas of Arizona. More than thirty herd areas were identified with the largest concentration in the northwestern and southwestern parts of the state. These numbers have stayed fairly steady over the last two decades.

As shown in the nearby illustration, the Black Mountains in northwest Arizona has the largest concentration of desert sheep in any one area. Numerous herds are also scattered throughout the southwest corner of the state with some of the largest groups in the Sierra Pintas and the Growler Mountains. These areas in a north-south corridor on the western side of Arizona are home to around 95 percent of the desert bighorn in the state.

Arizona has established itself as a leader in providing bighorn movement corridors over three highway overpasses. These projects have served as models for similar actions in other western states.

The recovery of the desert sheep populations in Arizona is a noted success story and exemplifies the restoration efforts in the western states. The state rivals California in desert sheep populations and is in the top tier of U.S. states for this game. From 2010-2011, more than $600,000 was generated from sheep-hunting permits to aid bighorn management programs. In 2023, 136 hunters drew permit-tags with a 96.3 percent success rate.

Baja California (North and South)

The Baja peninsula of Mexico includes the states of Baja California in the north and Baja California Sur in the south. These two Mexican states are home to two subspecies of desert sheep—Peninsular sheep (*Ovis canadensis cremnobates*) and Weems sheep (*Ovis canadensis weemsi*) with the Peninsular bighorns almost exclusively in the northern state and the Weems in the south.

Large herds of these sheep once roamed the peninsula with a combined estimate for these two subspecies of around 28,000 in the late 1920s. But the history of declining numbers for these sheep parallels those in the United States, except the Baja sheep's decimation came nearly a century later. From 1930 to 1975 the plentiful herds on the peninsula diminished to less than 3,000 sheep. Competition with feral livestock, disease, and virtually unregulated market and trophy hunting after 1931 led to this disheartening decline.

Further reductions in sheep numbers in the 1980s brought government intervention, and in 1990 the president of Mexico decreed a complete halt to sheep hunting throughout the Baja peninsula. By then the Peninsular bighorn population had been reduced to around 2,500, and the Weems numbers much lower. Hunting in Baja California Sur was re-opened after 1995 but the ban in the north state has continued to this day.

A privately funded effort to promote recovery of the Weems sheep began in 1995 with the translocation of 30 of these bighorns on predator-free Isla del Carmen near Loreto. Surplus population on the island was soon being relocated to formerly inhabited rangelands in the mountains. Current estimates of these sheep on Carmen are in the hundreds with 30 hunting permits sold annually, some as high as $90,000 each.

Carefully managed Weems hunts in 1997 and 1998 generated more than $500,000 for wildlife conservation and social projects in the southern state. The benefits of hunting to locals and a public education program led to reduced poaching and removal of much of the feral livestock on sheep ranges.

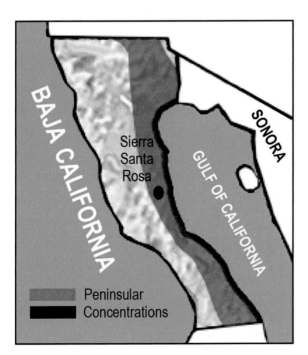

In addition, a nationally protected desert bighorn habitat was established within the Vizcaino Biosphere Reserve in 1988, the area where I hunted on the slopes of Las Tres Vírgenes volcanoes in 2019. By 2015, nearly $3 million had been produced from permits sold in this

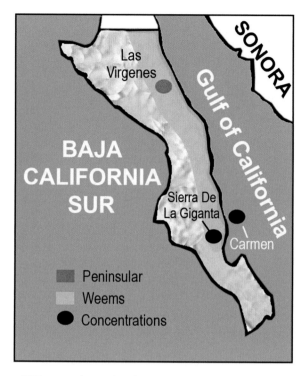

reserve.

By the year 2000, the Peninsular sheep population approached 2,500, and Weems numbers were stabilized at around 350. With the continued ban on sheep hunting in the north, these numbers of Peninsular sheep have likely improved. And the successful transplantation program on Isla del Carmen has further stabilized and likely increased the number of Weems sheep in the south.

Although the Weems numbers are still relatively small compared to the Peninsular numbers in the northern state, officials are guardedly optimistic that these numbers are growing. The $6 million in revenue generated from hunting permits in the southern state from 1996 to 2015 should go a long way toward restoration and conservation programs for these sheep.

California

Meat hunting during California's "gold rush" days and a large influx of settlers in the nineteenth century led to a more than 100-year ban on hunting all bighorn sheep in the Golden State. Driven by concerns over the vanishing desert bighorns, this 1878 moratorium by the California Legislature may have been the first bighorn hunting ban in the nation.

Even with this strict measure, the 97 identified herds of bighorns in California had declined to 61 by the mid-twentieth century, with

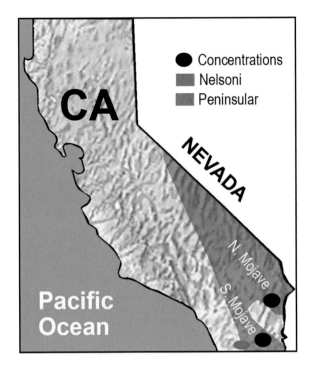

many of these herds greatly diminished in numbers. Following the hunting ban, disease epidemics from domestic livestock and alteration of water sources continued to take a large toll.

Of the ten "metapopulations" (spatially separated significant populations of the same species) of bighorn sheep in California, seven have been identified as desert bighorns. The "California bighorns" of the Sierra Nevada are a separate subspecies of *Ovis canadensis* and not classified as desert sheep. The Peninsular bighorns (*Ovis canadensis cremnobates)* of far southern California are a part of the desert population, but they are classed as a protected subspecies and hunting these sheep is prohibited.

With the state's inception of limited legal bighorn hunting in 1987, nearly $3 million in revenues has aided bighorn sheep management in California. Still, permits are scarce with only 22 draw tags and one fund-raiser tag for desert sheep in 2023. With permits divided between desert bighorn and California bighorn, hunting opportunities for both are limited.

Some 4,500 desert bighorn (*Ovis canadensis nelsoni)* were estimated in the state in 2003, and this increased to 5,200 by 2010. More than 5,100 were estimated in 2018, indicating a fairly stable population. All of these desert dwellers are in the far southern and southeastern sections of the state with a big part of them in the highlands of the Mojave Desert. Although California is estimated to have the third largest population of desert sheep of all U.S. states, hunting opportunities are greatly limited.

Colorado

Colorado is a prime example of introducing wild sheep into an area with habitat thought suitable but where no evidence of prior habitation existed. In the 1970s state wildlife managers believed that the low-elevations of western Colorado could support desert bighorn sheep, and in 1979 eleven sheep from southwestern Arizona (*Ovis canadensis mexicana*) were released into Devils Canyon just northwest of Grand Junction.

Two hundred more desert bighorn were subsequently released, and by 2001 nearly 500 sheep spread over four herds could be identified in western Colorado. Three of these herds were stable or increasing. Following a decline and comeback in the decade that followed, numbers of these sheep reached an all-time high in 2018 with an estimated population of 540 desert bighorns, mostly along the upper Delores River and in Dominquez Canyon.

Fifteen hunting tags were issued for desert bighorns in 2023, but officials have been cautious. Competition with widespread domestic sheep and goats in western Colorado are an ongoing concern. Some wildlife officials are skeptical of programs introducing wild sheep into seemingly suitable areas without evidence of prior habitation, yet western Colorado may be an area like that of the western Oklahoma Panhandle. Here wildlife officials discounted the possibility of wild sheep ever living in the canyons and mesas of the Panhandle. But a longtime rancher

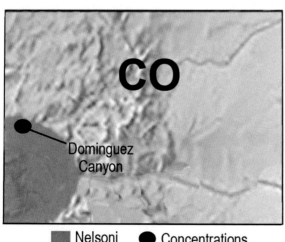

Nelsoni   ● Concentrations

This mature desert ram was photographed atop Oklahoma's state highpoint, Black Mesa, in June 2024.

west of the town of Boise City surprised officials with ancient pictographs of wild sheep along the banks of the Cimarron River on his ranchlands.

In 2012 a carcass of a bighorn was found on Black Mesa—a lava-formed plateau in the northwest corner of the Panhandle abutting the Colorado line. Since then, numerous hikers on this state highpoint have reported viewing wild sheep on the slopes of the mesa. State officials believe these bighorns are migrating from southern Colorado onto what was thought to be an unsuitable range for these sheep. But in the Oklahoman Panhandle, and in western Colorado, the inability of officials to document past habitation obviously doesn't preclude the possibility. If the range is suitable, they apparently will return on their own or thrive when transplanted.

Nevada

Nevada boasts of more desert bighorn sheep than any of the lower-48 states and is arguably the biggest success story in the restoration of this iconic game animal. Native pictographs and petroglyphs are plentiful throughout southern Nevada, ancient evidence of thriving bighorn herds in past history. But that was well before the widespread mining and settlement of the last half of the nineteenth century.

Meat hunting and competition for the lifesaving springs and seeps of the arid landscape decimated the wild sheep populations into the twentieth century. Even with the ban on hunting bighorns in 1917, continued decline reduced the states wild sheep population to an estimated 700 to 1,000 by 1940. By then, only a dozen beleaguered herds could be found in the mountain ranges of southern Nevada.

The Nevada Fish and Game Commission prioritized the rebuilding of the desert bighorn herds after World War II, and limited hunting was reinstated in 1952, some 35 years after its ban. Harvest regulations focused on the taking of trophy rams and remained highly restrictive. Support by sportsmen for increased hunting opportunities led to the introduction in 1967 of bighorns from California to dry rangelands in northern Nevada.

The success of these efforts by Nevada wildlife officials was

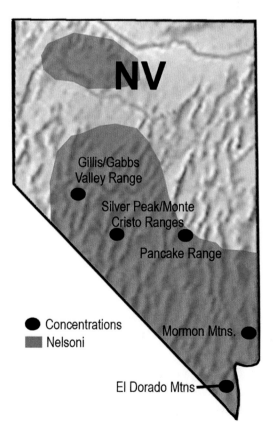

encouraging and soon led to the relocation of desert sheep in other formerly inhabited areas of the state. State and federal officials combined in a concerted program of restoration. Much of the funding for restoration and relocation came from sportsmen, many wanting increased trophy opportunities and willing to volunteer time and resources to aid state officials in meeting conservation objectives. By 2012, Nevada's herds were estimated to contain more than 5,000 sheep, and 281 hunting permits were issued with a success rate of 86 percent.

This bighorn that I took in Nevada stands proudly in my game room in Oklahoma City.

I took advantage of one of those hunting opportunities in 2013 with a hunt north of the Jackson Mountains in northwestern Nevada. I was able to select one of those bighorn transplants from California from a large herd of about fifty in Calavera Canyon. This trophy ram was about 12-years-old and to this day stands proudly as a full-mount in my game room. It was at that 2013 hunt when I first learned that Nevada could by then boast of more wild sheep than any other state but Alaska.

Momentum from Nevada's success continued with more relocations and reintroductions. By 2019 estimates of bighorn sheep in Nevada had mushroomed to around 12,000. Much of the recent restoration efforts have been in the vast Desert National Wildlife Refuge (DNWR) of southern Nevada, first established in 1936 to preserve the bighorn sheep and their habitat. Located just north of Las Vegas, DNWR is the largest U.S. wildlife refuge outside of Alaska and protects the largest population of desert bighorn in the Mojave Desert, which spans the nation's four southwestern states. It is one of four refuges in Nevada with the same goal of protecting desert bighorn.

Still, disease and drought brought a significant decline in the state's wild sheep populations after 2019. The 2023 estimate of less than 10,000 bighorn sheep reflects this setback. The state is moving forward with recovery efforts, however, and have learned new strategies to deal with "die-offs" like that of recent years. Despite the decline from 2019 to 2023, more than 300 permits were issues for rams and ewes in 2023.

New Mexico

Desert bighorns in the future state of New Mexico were first reported by Spanish explorer Francisco Vázquez de Coronado in 1540. Those sheep seen by the Spanish gold seeker in the Zuni Mountains in the northwest region of the state were typical of the widespread desert bighorn herds throughout the dry mountain ranges in the central and southern regions of current-day New Mexico.

Competition and disease from domestic livestock and meat hunting had limited these herds (*Ovis canadensis mexicana*) by the mid-twentieth century to only the San Andreas and Hatchet Mountains in the southwest corner of the state. Despite the state's sheep hunting ban in 1889, poaching, domestic sheep herds, and cattle ranching nearly eradicated the desert dwellers.

Department of Game and Fish officials began a bighorn propagation program at Red Rock Wildlife Area north of Lordsburg

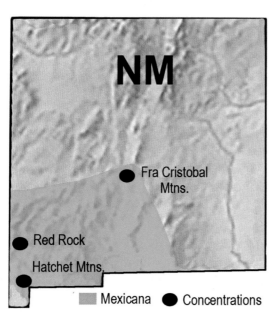

in 1972, translocating 22 desert bighorns from the San Andreas Mountains and from the Mexican state of Sonora. The meager numbers of these sheep resulted in the listing of these bighorns as "endangered" in 1980 following a scabies mite infestation.

By 1990 the number of desert bighorn was estimated in the low hundreds. Aided by efforts to control mountain lions in Red Rock, by the late 1990s some 200 surplus desert sheep were translocated from this wildlife area to augment and reestablish herds in former habitats.

Mountain lions have continued to be especially detrimental to New Mexican bighorns. As high as 85 percent of deaths of radio-collared bighorn are attributed to mountain lion predation. Sport hunting of mountain lions in the state has been generally ineffective.

By 2011 the population of desert bighorn had recovered some-what from the disastrous scabies mite infestation, and a statewide hunting program began in 2012 with 21 permits on six units. The raffle and auction permits began generating $200,000 annually with another $50,000 from public hunting tags. A permit in 2013 sold through the Wild Sheep Foundation for an astounding $180,000! The high cost of tags for out-of-staters has recently been generating several million dollars annually through the bighorn tag drawing process. Some of these funds have been used to develop a mountain lion control program.

The translocation program from the 1,500-acre Red Rock Wild-life Area has continued with some success. By 2018 desert bighorn estimates were up to around 1,200 in the state. In 2023, 28 permits were issued for desert rams with a 100 percent success rate.

Sonora, Mexico

The isolated mountain ranges in northwest Sonora have long been a stronghold for desert bighorn sheep, whose populations have prob-ably never been critically low in this northern Mexican state. Nearly all of these mountainous areas of northwest Sonora along the Gulf of California have been home to sizeable populations of sheep and a venue for sport hunters.

The remoteness of this rugged, thornscrub-covered region im-peded reliable estimates of desert bighorn throughout much of the twentieth century. Conservative estimates of these sheep centered around 1,000. As concern for these animals grew in the 1990s, a number of official surveys were taken, each confirming a sizeable native population of bighorns throughout the northwest mountain ranges.

An analysis of these various surveys produced a still somewhat conservative estimate of as high as 2,000 desert bighorns by 1999. These numbers were large enough to easily support a limited sport hunting program with proceeds for both bighorn conservation and other wildlife in the state.

The Sonoran bighorns are mostly native to various mountain ranges, but in 1976 a small herd of 19 of these sheep were transplanted from the mainland to Isla Tiburon. With 1,200 square miles of uninhabited land, Tiburon is the largest island in Mexico and directly west of the city of Hermosillo in west-central Sonora. It had been set aside as a nature reserve in 1963.

Much like that of the nearby Isla del Carmen off the coast of Baja California Sur, the Tiburon transplant program has been a huge success. Since the late 1970s, more than 500 bighorns have been relocated, many to areas in Mexico where bighorn sheep had long been extirpated—Chihuahua, Coahuila, and Nuevo Leon. Even with these exports, the Tiburon has maintained a population of over 500 sheep.

Factors limiting the still sizeable sheep populations in Sonora before the twenty-first century were widespread poaching by poor families and disease from local domestic stock. The last couple of decades has seen a growing awareness among Sonoran natives of the potential for additional income from sheep hunters. This has brought new protections for these bighorns by landowners.

Estimates of

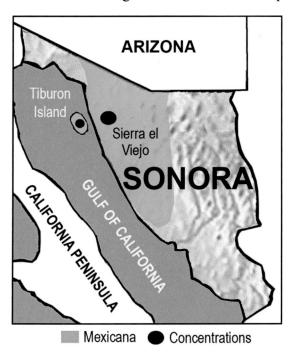

free-ranging desert bighorns on mainland Sonora in 2015 were as high as 2,300. Adding in those on Tiburon brings the total in the state closer to 3,000, a healthy population that appears stable if not growing.

The income from hunting permits has the attention of local landowners who are accommodating hunters from all over North America. And the high desert of northwest Sonora provides a great setting for a sheep hunt, ruggedly beautiful and plenty challenging. I can personally attest to a good experience from my own sheep hunting adventure in Sonora in 2014. (See Chapter 3 above.)

In Mexican states outside Sonora and the Baja peninsula, desert sheep were extirpated by the 1960s. These areas included the northern Mexico states of Chihuahua, Coahuila and Nuevo Leon. But with the success of the Mexican transplant programs, the states of Chihuahua and Coahuila have restored small herds of desert bighorn and have begun limited permit hunting. A private facility in Nuevo Leon was stocked with fifty bighorns in 2015, so this state may also begin limited permitting, if it hasn't already. Future generations of sheep hunters may someday visit these three states in Mexico at levels rivaling the Baja peninsula and Sonora.

Texas

The near extirpation of wild sheep from Texas by the middle of the twentieth century has been followed by one of the most successful conservation success stories in North America. The estimated herds numbering some 1,500 sheep in 1880s west Texas have been restored by the remarkable transplant programs of an extensive public/private partnership.

The remoteness of the rugged rangelands west of the Pecos River in west Texas had experienced limited settlement from the East, and the bighorn herds were relatively stable until the arrival of the railway in 1881. Market hunters took advantage of the unregulated harvesting of these sheep, providing meat to the newly arrived railroad workers and miners. The 1903 ban on hunting desert bighorns in Texas came too late for most of the dwindling herds. The 300 or so bighorns estimated in the late 1930s were further decimated by the arrival of domestic sheep in the early 1940s. The last pair of native bighorns were sighted in 1960 in the Sierra Diablo mountains just north of Van Horn.

A reintroduction project in the 1950s combined the efforts of the U.S. Fish and Wildlife Service, Boone and Crockett Club, The Wildlife Management Institute, and state wildlife officials from both Texas and Arizona. Sixteen bighorns (*Ovis canadensis mexicana*) from Arizona's Kofa Game Range were reintroduced in the late 1950s to a 427-acre "brood pasture" on the Black Gap Wildlife Management Area just northeast of Big Bend National Park. The population had increased to 84 bighorns by 1971, but disease and predation by mountain lions took a toll.

In 1983 an additional refuge for the sheep was constructed at Sierra Diablo Wildlife Management Area, and 17 bighorns from Nevada were reintroduced. A dozen more bighorns from Utah and Arizona were added in the 1980s, and by 1998 the Sierra Diablo site had grown to almost 200 free-ranging sheep. The success of this project led to an in-state transplant of 20 bighorns from Sierra Diablo to the Elephant Mountain Wildlife Management Area in 1987.

In-state transplants became the rule in Texas in the 1990s and afterward, and a record 46 bighorns were relocated from Elephant Mountain to Big Bend Ranch State Park in 2010. The success of the Texas

reintroduction programs has eliminated the need for any captive breeding facilities in the state. The 1,500 or so Texas bighorns now in the western areas of the state wander on their rangelands as freely as the west Texas wind.

It should be noted that the Texas private landowners (more than 96 percent of the state is in private hands) played a big role in this remarkable comeback of bighorns. Sale of landowner permits to hunt bighorns can be lucrative, and ranchers have readily cooperated with government officials to promote this reintroduction of sheep and to protect them. Landowners work to control mountain lions and the detrimental effects of the thriving herds of aoudad in west Texas, which are in direct competition with the wild sheep for grazing lands and water.

Limited permit hunting began in 1990, and by 2013 was up to 17 tags, 14 on private ranches and three on public lands. Ten hunting tags auctioned over the years by the Wild Sheep Foundation brought in more than $1 million for bighorn management in the state by 2014.

I hunted with a private landowner tag in 2010 and 2011 on a ranch near the Black Gap Wildlife Management Area northeast of Big Bend National Park. This was my first desert sheep hunt, and I had quite a time of it—as you may have read earlier in Chapter 2 of this book. I learned a lot and am grateful for the opportunity and the experience.

Utah

Utah has a bighorn conservation success story that rivals that of Texas. When Spanish priest Silvestre Vélez de Escalante explored the northern fringes of the Spanish empire in the New World in 1776, he wrote that "wild sheep live in such abundance that their tracks are like those of great herds of domestic sheep." But the vast herds that Escalante saw around the Colorado River in present-day southeast Utah would all but vanish by the 1960s.

The settlement of Utah brought unregulated hunting of bighorns and competition and disease from domestic livestock that continued well into the twentieth century. By 1960 the only wild sheep in the state were a remnant herd of desert bighorns along the Colorado River in the southeastern corner. Bighorn sheep were reintroduced to areas in the state beginning with Rocky Mountain bighorns near Brigham City in northern Utah in 1966, followed by desert bighorns in Zion National Park in 1973. Further restoration efforts led to nearly 2,000 bighorns transplanted to areas of historical habitation over the next four decades, including the relocation of an estimated 850 desert bighorns.

By the end of the 1990s, several million acres of public land in southeastern and southern Utah were designated a "natural area," providing protections to desert sheep in these regions. While these protected areas provide good habitat for the sheep, there has been some concern that this designation also limits management options in these lands, including a prohibition on the development of water holes.

UTAH

N. San Rafael
S. San Rafael
Island in the Sky/Potash
Escalante

◼ Nelsoni   ● Concentrations

Despite an increase in recreational activity in the Utah desert bighorns' southeastern stronghold and continued transmission of disease from domestic livestock, officials estimated a population of nearly 3,000 desert sheep by 2018. They live mostly in the state's hot, dry canyonlands in the southeast's "red rock" country. This marks a remarkable turnaround for these populations, and a corresponding increase in bighorn hunting opportunities in the state beginning with 10 desert bighorn permits in 1967.

Bighorn sheep are managed as a once-in-a-lifetime game in the state, and competition for hunting permits has been fierce over the last few decades. A high of 54 permits for desert sheep were issued in 2011. From 1967 to 2012, more than 1,000 permits for desert bighorn hunts have been issued with an 82 percent success rate. In 2024 more than 21,000 hunters applied for 69 public-draw desert bighorn permits.

Enhanced Hunting Opportunities

The three-fold increase in North American desert sheep since 1960 has seen a marked increase in hunting permits for this prized game. As described in this chapter, the controlled harvesting of these animals and funding for conservation efforts have gone hand in hand. A thoughtful, cooperative effort of all stakeholders—government officials, private groups and hunters—in the conservation of these desert icons has led both to a significant restoration of these wild sheep and more opportunities for outdoor sportsmen.

The coming generations of stakeholders in these conservation efforts need only look at the past half century of success to guide future programs. Wild sheep relocations, re-introductions and introductions in supportive habitat have all been a part of this success story. Overseeing these efforts has required a dedicated, knowledgeable base of wildlife officials supported by an array of public-private organizations. And carefully regulated hunting of desert bighorns has not slowed the progress in restoring the numbers of these sheep. In fact, the revenues from the hunting of this game have played a significant role in this progress.

The regulated hunting of desert sheep varies widely from state to

Hunting opportunities for desert bighorn sheep, or any North American wild sheep, have not been this good since the 19th century. Most of this is owed to the cooperation between government officials, private groups and hunters.

state, ranging from a continued ban in some states to an increasing number of permits in others. The trend has been toward more permits and more hunting in more locations—a reflection of the success of the restoration and conservation efforts of the twentieth century.

Still, the process of acquiring a permit and following the hunting regulations in a given state requires current and accurate information. The next chapter in this book is meant to provide the informational resources for outdoor sportsmen who hope to enjoy the challenge of a hunting a desert bighorn in its natural habitat.

CHAPTER 7

Planning Your Desert Bighorn Adventure
(Hunting Licenses, Tag Requirements
& Annual Deadlines)

If you're still with me at this point in the book, you're likely considering a desert bighorn hunt. This chapter is all about taking the
final steps for hunting desert sheep.

Earlier in this book we looked at the history of desert bighorns
in various U.S. and Mexican states, including their decline and their
return in significant numbers. We've also reviewed where these
sheep can be found in these states. But where they can be found and
where they can be hunted do not always correlate. Where they can
be hunted, when they can be hunted, and how a hunter gets a permit
to hunt them varies from state to state.

The following in this chapter provides guidance on how to begin
the process of planning and obtaining a permit for a desert sheep
hunt in North America. Much of the information for this process is
provided by the various states' parks and wildlife websites. I know,
I know—many of you over-50 types like me don't yearn to sit in
front of a computer screen and try to figure out what the hell you're
supposed to click next. But some computer work will be necessary.

Outfitters, Organizations and Publications

An alternative to doing your own research for a sheep hunt in a given state is to contact an outfitter first. Many outfitters can provide you with a permit (for a price, of course) or at least get you on down the road to start your application process. Contact information for outfitters who work with sheep hunters can be found in several publications, including the quarterly *Slam Quest* (published by Grand Slam Club Ovis) and the quarterly *Wild Sheep* (published by The Wild Sheep Foundation). In additional to outfitter ads and information, these glossy publications have great write-ups on sheep hunts and other articles of interest to a sheep hunter.

Joining the above two organizations that produce these periodicals provides you with a subscription, but your membership will also allow important networking opportunities. Yes, you'll have to pay for these memberships, but good information about anything rarely comes free. If you're serious about hunting wild sheep, I think you'll find joining one or both of these organizations well worth the dues. Their publications alone are probably worth your joining fees.

Linking with these organizations and contacting outfitters could be a good way to jump-start your hunting plans, but you may still need to obtain your hunting license and apply for a tag through one of the state's websites. This chapter provides an overview by state on the how, where and when to hunt bighorn desert sheep in 2024. While some of these specifications will change in coming years, few states make drastic changes over short periods. And if they do, the online links and contact information on these pages should help a sheep hunter stay abreast of these changes. Thus, the information provided here should be useful for some time to come.

In the rest of this chapter, I've tried to make this process a little less painful for you by previewing these state wildlife department websites and listing the key links to the information you may be looking for. I also provide a brief overview of what you can expect as you begin wading through these rules and requirements. If it gets too frustrating for you online, you can call a wildlife official using one of the phone numbers provided herein.

Regional office locations and phone numbers were listed only for offices in these states near desert sheep and likely to be contacted for information relevant to hunting this game.

ARIZONA
Licensing and Permitting

AZ Game and Fish Depart. Website Home Page: www.azgfd.com
Phone Number: (602) 942-3000
Mailing Address: 5000 W. Carefree Highway, Phoenix AZ 85086-5000

Office Locations

Main Office – Phoenix
Arizona Game and Fish Department
5000 W. Carefree Highway
Phoenix, AZ 85086-5000
(602) 942-3000

Region IV – Yuma
9140 E. 28th St.
Yuma, AZ 85365
(928) 342-0091

Region I – Pinetop
2878 E. White Mountain Blvd.
Pinetop, AZ 85935
(928) 367-4281

Region V – Tucson
555 N. Greasewood Rd.
Tucson, AZ 85745
(520) 628-5376

Region II – Flagstaff
3500 S. Lake Mary Road
Flagstaff, AZ 86001
(928) 774-5045

Region VI – Mesa
7200 E. University
Mesa, AZ 85207
(480) 981-9400

Key Arizona Game and Fish Department Website Links

Home Page ....azgfd.com
Hunting Regs Publication ....azgfd.com/hunting/regulations/
Hunter Portal Account.....................accounts.azgfd.com
Hunt Draw and License .... azgfd.com/hunting/hunt-draw-and-licenses/
Draw Application............................ draw.azgfd.com
Draw Odds and Harvest Data ...... azgfd.com/surveydata
Bonus Points ....azgfd.com/bonuspoint
Protecting Bonus Pts.................... azgfd.com/pointguard

Arizona Sheep Hunting Overview
(2024-2025)

Arizona hunting regulations can be downloaded as a publication in PDF format from the AZ Game and Fish Department website. This publication includes the annual regulations for statewide hunting of bighorn sheep and other game (see link previous page).

As in all U.S. states, a hunting license and hunt-permit tag are required to hunt bighorn sheep in Arizona. Arizona licenses can be purchased online and will not be mailed. Purchasers can print their license from their home computer. Licenses may also be purchased from a license dealer or at any Arizona Game and Fish Department office (locations above).

Residents can purchase a general hunting license for $37 and a bighorn sheep permit-tag for $313 (includes $13 app fee). Non-residents are required to purchase a combination hunting and fishing license for $160 and a bighorn sheep permit-tag for $1,815 (includes a $15 app fee). Sheep permit tags are issued via random drawing, and eligible applicants must have a valid Arizona hunting license on the last day of the app deadline for draw eligibility.

Individuals applying for a bighorn sheep permit must apply online by the deadline specified in the Hunt Permit-tag Application Schedule (deadline for 2024 was June 4). Step-by-step instructions can be found on the department's website. The permit application service

---

2023 Desert Bighorn Draw Results in Arizona

Hunting Units	First Choice Applicants	Issued
44	22,055	137

2023 Desert Bighorn Harvest Summary in Arizona

Harvest	Hunters	% Successful
131	136	96.3

In addition to the above in 2023, Arizona auctioned two special tags for a desert bighorn; the two special tag-permits were successful.

169

will generally be available online by early to mid May. The department's website will post updates on availability. Applicants should ensure their credit card payment information is current, as a payment decline voids the application for that year.

Draw results are available online through the applicant's free portal account (created by the applicant on the department website). Tags for successful draws will be mailed within 10-15 business days. The Arizona E-Tag app (available from Apple or Google Play) allows real-time delivery of digital licenses and tags. Tag permit payments are immediately refunded for unsuccessful applications, and a bonus point is awarded for future draws. Each bonus point equates to one extra application in the draw, thus increasing a draw applicant's chances for a future permit.

The general season for hunting bighorn sheep in Arizona is October 1 through December 31, but the season varies by unit. A few units start as early as October 1 and run through December 31. Most range from sometime in November or early December through December 31.

Desert bighorn ewes and juveniles at the edge of the Superstition Mountains overlooking the sprawling city of Phoenix.

CALIFORNIA
Licensing and Permitting

CA Dept. of Fish and Wildlife Website Home Page: www.wildlife.ca.gov
Phone Number: (916) 445-0411
Mailing Address: 715 P Street, Sacramento CA 95814

OFFICE LOCATIONS

NORTHERN REGION
Redding Office
601 Locust Street
Redding, CA 9600
(530) 225-2300
AskRegion1@wildlife.ca.gov

BAY DELTA REGION
Fairfield Office
2825 Cordelia Rd #100
Fairfield, CA 94534
(707) 428-2002
AskBDR@wildlife.ca.gov

Eureka Field Office
619 Second Street
Eureka, CA 95501
(707) 445-6493

Stockton Field Office
2109 Arch Airport Rd #100
Stockton CA 95206
(209) 234-3420

NORTH CENTRAL REGION
1701 Nimbus Rd,
Rancho Cordova, CA 95670
(916) 358-2900
R2Info@wildlife.ca.gov

SOUTH COAST REGION
3883 Ruffin Road
San Diego, CA 92123
(858) 467-4201
AskR5@wildlife.ca.gov

CENTRAL REGION
1234 E. Shaw Avenue
Fresno, CA 93710
(559) 243-4005
Reg4Assistant@wildlife.ca.gov

INLAND DESERTS REGION
3602 Inland Empire Blvd., C-220
Ontario, CA 91764
(909) 484-0167
AskRegion6@wildlife.ca.gov

Key California Dept. of Fish and Wildlife Website Links

Home Page .... wildlife.ca.gov/
Big Game Hunting Digest .... wildlife.ca.gov/Publications/Hunting-Digest
Hunting License....................... wildlife.ca.gov/Licensing/Hunting
Sheep Hunt Tags.................... wildlife.ca.gov/Licensing/Hunting/Big-Game

171

California Sheep Hunting Overview
(2024-2025)

A useful publication for big-game hunters titled *California Big Game Digest (2024-2025)* could be found on the California Fish and Wildlife website (see web address above) as a downloadable PDF in 2024. This had a range of information hunters in the Golden State would need including key information for desert sheep hunters.

A valid, fiscal-year (July 1–June 30) California hunting license is required, as the 1-Day and 2-Day Nonresident California Hunting License is not valid for hunting bighorn sheep. Full-year licenses can be purchased online through the department's website, at any department license sales office, or through a license agent. Resident licenses in 2024 were $61.82 and $216.00 for non-residents.

Purchasers of a California fishing or hunting license, permits, or annual passes must create a customer record and obtain a Get Outdoors Identification (GO ID) number through the department's website. The GO ID will print on all licenses and is used to help track purchases, preference points, and harvest reporting requirements.

Hunting license applicants must present evidence of having held a California hunting license in a previous period; or having completed California-approved hunter education; or holding a current hunting license or one issued in either of the two previous years from any state, province, European Union country or South Africa. (More details can be found in the Big Game Hunting Digest.)

2023 Desert Bighorn Draw Results in California

Hunting Units	Total Applicants	Permits Issued
10	7,318	23

2023 Desert Bighorn Harvest Summary in California

Harvest	Hunters	% Successful
17	23	73.9

The fee for entering the Big Game Drawing for a sheep permit is $8.13 for residents and non-residents. Permit-tags for sheep in 2004 were $535.50 for residents and $1,986.75 for non-residents. Previous draw winners were ineligible in future draws. In 2024, all transactions for drawing entries were to be completed by midnight, June 2, and applicants for "preference points only" had the same deadline.

California's drawing works under a "modified preference point system" with tag quotas split into two groups: one group by preference points and the other awarded in "draw-by-choice" drawings. (Details in the *California Big Game Hunting Digest*.)

The department took 10 business days to complete the draw after the June 2 application deadline. Applicants could look up their drawing results online about two weeks after June 2. Successful sheep-draw applicants were to have received their payment notices in the mail by July 2. Payments by successful tag applicants were due by July 15. Unsuccessful applicants were not notified.

In 2024, California held drawings for a few desert sheep permits in most of its 10 sheep-hunting zones. The northern-most, Zone 7, is just east of Bishop, but the other nine zones cluster in the southeast ranging north and south of a line between Needles and Barstow.

Hunting season for desert sheep in California for most zones in 2024 was from December 7 to February 2.

Nelson bighorn photographed at California's Anza-Borrego Desert State Park, south of the city of Palm Desert and abutting the west side of the Salton Sea.

COLORADO
Licensing and Permitting

Colorado Parks and Wildlife Website Home Page: cpw.state.co.us/
Phone Number: (303) 297-1192
Mailing Address: 6060 Broadway, Denver CO 80216

SOUTHWEST REGION

Durango Office
151 E. 16th Street
Durango, CO 81303
(970) 247-0855

Lamar Office
2500 S. Main Street
Lamar, CO 81052
(719) 336-6600

Gunnison Office
300 W. New York Ave.
Gunnison, CO 81230
(970) 641-7060

Monte Vista Office
0722 South Road 1 East
Monte Vista, CO 81144
(719) 587-6900

Montrose Office
2300 S. Townsend Ave.
Montrose, CO 81401
(970) 252-6000

Key Colorado Parks and Wildlife Website Links
Home Page................... cpw.state.co.us/
Sheep Hunt Brochure.....https://cpw.widen.net/s/m27g5rnwwq/
colorado-sheep-and-goat-brochure
Hunting Information.......cpw.state.co.us/hunting
Big-Game Lic. App........cpw.state.co.us/hunting/big-game

Colorado Sheep Hunting Overview
(2024-2025)

Reflecting the sparse desert sheep herds in only the southwest and west-central parts of the state, Colorado offers very limited opportunities for hunting desert sheep. Nonetheless, an annual desert sheep draw was offered in 2024 and the numbers may increase in the future. You will first need to set up an online account, which you could find instructions for on the Parks and Wildlife website.

In 2024 no separate charge for a permit to hunt sheep was assessed as this charge was included in the state license for hunting desert sheep. In 2024 this license was $366.13 for residents and $2,686.04 for non-residents. In addition, a non-refundable habitat stamp of $12.15 is charged along with a non-refundable license application fee of $8.00 for residents and $366.13 for non-residents. The larger charge for the license is assessed only if the applicant is drawn for a sheep.

A hunter education card is needed to apply for a hunting license in Colorado for those born after Jan. 1, 1949. Individuals over 50 and U.S. active military or veterans may obtain a hunter education certificate by testing out: cpw.info/hunter-education-test-out.

In 2024 applications to hunt sheep were accepted online or by phone at 1-800-244-5613, starting March 1 and ending April 2. About two weeks after the close of applications, emails were sent to successful applicants. Payment deadline for the license was April 30,

---

2023 Desert Bighorn Draw Results in Colorado

Hunting Units	First Choice Applicants	Issued
4	5,541	15

2023 Desert Bighorn Harvest Summary in Colorado

Harvest	Hunters	% Successful
15	15	100.0

175

and failure to make payment resulted in forfeiture of the successful draw and any preference points used for the draw.

In 2024, 14 resident licenses (permits) were drawn for 14 desert rams, but only one resident license (permit) was drawn for non-residents.

Colorado Parks and Wildlife provided an excellent small publication titled Sheep Hunt Brochure (see web link above) that could be downloaded. This brochure provided detailed guidance for hopeful Colorado sheep hunters.

Resident licenses were drawn in four hunting zones in Colorado for 2024. Non-residents could hunt in only one of these zones. The desert sheep hunting season ran from Nov. 1-30.

Bighorn ram in the Colorado National Monument, a unit of the National Park Service near the state's western city of Grand Junction. Within the desert lands of the Colorado Plateau, the park is noted for its high canyon walls and striking rock formations of granite.

NEVADA
Licensing and Permitting

Nevada Dept. of Wildlife Website Home Page: https://www.ndow.org
Game Management Phone Number: (775) 688-1523

OFFICE LOCATIONS

WESTERN REGION
1100 Valley Road
Reno, NV 89512
(775) 688-1506

EASTERN REGION
60 Youth Center Road
Elko, NV 89801
(775) 777-2300

Fallon Office
380 West B. Street
Fallon, NV 89406
(775) 423-3171

Ely Office
1218 North Alpha Street
Ely, NV 89301
(775) 289-1655 ext. 21

Winnemucca Office
705 East Fourth Street
Winnemucca, NV 89445
(775) 623-6565

SOUTHERN REGION
3373 Pepper Lane
Las Vegas, NV 89120
(702) 486-5127

Key Nevada Dept. of Wildlife Website Links
Home Page .... ndow.org
Hunting Rules & Regs ... ndow.org/get-outside/hunting/rules-regulations/
Hunt Licensing................ ndowlicensing.com
Big Game App Process...ndow.org/apply-buy/apply-buy-hunting/#
Sheep Hunt Info .... eregulations.com/nevada/hunting/bighorn-sheep-hunts
General Big Game Info....eregulations.com/assets/docs/resources/NV/24NVBG_LR2.pdf

Nevada Sheep Hunting Overview
(2023-2024)

Nevada's large desert sheep population currently offers a bigger annual permit quota than any other state, with a random permit-tag draw for both rams and ewes. Like many other states currently, an excellent downloadable PDF is available to provide necessary information for would-be sheep hunters in Nevada. Titled *Nevada Big Game Seasons and Applications* in 2024, the PDF could be downloaded to your home computer from the state's wildlife department website (see link above for General Big Game Information).

Resident hunting licenses in 2024 were $75 per year, and $155 for non-residents. A non-refundable tag application fee of $10 is required for entering the draw for a sheep tag. Resident sheep tags are $120, and $1,200 for non-residents. If an applicant is not drawn, the hunting license fee is refunded.

Those born after January 1, 1960, were required to provide proof of hunter education for purchase of a Nevada hunting license. Proof can be provided with an official hunter education card or certificate from any state or Canadian province, with the hunter education number and state or provincial logo or seal or a previous year's hunting license with the hunter education number or mark.

The main permit-tag application period for big game generally ran from mid-March to mid-May. Some special tags are offered, including Heritage Tags, through bidding auctions, and Dream tags through raffle-style drawings. Results from the main draw are available at the end of May or beginning of June. Application is online through the department's website. Residents and nonresidents

	Demand	Unique Apps	Quota	Tags Issued	Successful Hunters	% Success
2023 Desert Bighorn Draw Results in Nevada						
Rams	41,247	122,739	234	234	192	86.8
Ewes	2,352	3,613	89	90	44	56.4

can purchase a bonus point or automatically receive a bonus point for an unsuccessful big game tag application.

Quotas for desert bighorn sheep are distributed across dozens of hunting units throughout the state. Most of these are for desert rams, but 90 permits for desert ewes were awarded in 2023. In 2024, the season started as early as September 10-15 in a few units and usually ended on January 1 for most. Most of the 2024 desert sheep season in Nevada ran from November 20 through January 1.

In 2013, I was surprised to learn that Nevada had the largest bighorn sheep population of any of the lower-48 states. I took this 12-year-old bighorn prize northwest of Winnemucca.

NEW MEXICO
Licensing and Permitting

New Mexico Dept. of Game & Fish Website Home Page: wildlife.state.nm.us
Customer Service (toll-free): (888) 248-6866

OFFICE LOCATIONS

NORTHWEST OFFICE
7816 Alamo Road NW
Albuquerque, NM 87120
(505) 222-4700

SOUTHWEST OFFICE
2715 Northrise Drive
Las Cruces, NM 88011
(575) 532-2100

NORTHEAST OFFICE
215 York Canyon Road
PO Box 1145
Raton, NM 87740
(575) 445-2311

SOUTHEAST OFFICE
1615 W. College Blvd.
Roswell, NM 88201
(575) 624-6135

Key New Mexico Dept. of Game & Fish Website Links

Home Page .... wildlife.state.nm.us
Hunting Lic. & Permits....wildlife.state.nm.us/hunting/licenses-and-permits/
Draw Hunt Info.................wildlife.state.nm.us/hunting/applications-and-draw-information/
Bighorn Sheep Info. ....wildlife.state.nm.us/hunting/information-by-animal/big-game/
bighorn-sheep/
Hunting Maps................. wildlife.state.nm.us/hunting/maps/
Hunting Rules & Information Publication (downloadable):
wildlife.dgf.nm.gov/download/2024-2025-new-mexico-hunting-rules-and-info/

New Mexico Sheep Hunting Overview
(2023-2024)

Desert sheep hunting in New Mexico in 2022-2023 was exclusively in the southwestern and south-central parts of the state in six game-management units. Twenty-six desert ram permits were issued in 2022-2023 with an outstanding 100 percent success rate. Information for sheep hunters in New Mexico can be found in the downloadable publication *New Mexico Hunting Rules and Info* on the Game & Fish Department's website (see Hunting Rules & Info link above).

The state offered a bighorn sheep draw license-tag with residents paying $160 for a ram and $85 for a ewe (ewe hunts were limited to Rocky Mountain sheep). Non-residents were assessed $3,173 for a ram or ewe draw license-tag. A small non-refundable application fee also applied, $7 for residents and $13 for non-residents.

 Application fees and license-tag charges were assessed at the time the application was submitted with unsuccessful draw license-tags refunded. Successful draw licenses were mailed unless an E-Tag option was chosen by the applicant. New Mexico grants no preferences to previously unsuccessful applicants. State law reserves 84 percent of permits to residents.

Twenty-six permits for desert rams were drawn in 2024. Of the 26 permits for desert rams in 2022-2023, two were on private land

---

2023 Desert Bighorn Hunt Summary in New Mexico

2023 Permit Apps for Desert Ram Hunts

1st Choice	2nd Choice	3rd Choice	Total
5,309	5,849	488	11,646

Permits	Hunters*	Harvest*	% Successful
28	28	28	100.0

*Two of these were by auction or raffle.

---

and the rest on public. Population management hunts for bighorns may be available to unsuccessful draw applicants. New Mexico is a "one-and-done" state with hunters limited to one desert ram and one Rocky Mountain ram in their lifetimes.

The deadline for the sheep license draw in 2024 was March 20. Hunters could apply for up to three bighorn sheep hunt codes in the same year. Desert sheep season started as early as September 13 in one unit and ran as late as January 3 in another. The season spanned only two weeks in each of the 13 game-management units.

Jornada Mogollon Native Americans chipped into stone this scene from their successful desert bighorn hunt from a thousand years ago at a site near Alamogordo, New Mexico. Pictographs and petroglyphs of bighorn sheep can be found throughout the western United States with many of these portrayals in areas now devoid of this once-plentiful game.

TEXAS
Licensing and Permitting

Texas Parks and Wildlife Website Home Page: tpwd.texas.gov/
(800) 792-1112

Wildlife Division
4200 Smith School Road
Austin, TX 78744

Big Game Program
(830) 480-4038

Texas Parks & Wildlife Dept
Regional and Field Law Enforcement Offices

El Paso
401 East Franklin, Suite 520
El Paso, TX 79901
(915) 834-7050

Midland
4500 West Illinois, Suite 307
Midland, TX 79703
(432) 520-4649

Laredo
5119 Bob Bullock Loop
Laredo, TX 78041
(956) 718-1087

San Angelo
3407 South Chadbourne
San Angelo, TX 76904
(325) 651-4844

Lubbock
1702 Landmark Lane, Suite 1
Lubbock, TX 79415
(806) 761-4930

San Antonio
2391 N.E. Loop 410, Suite 409
San Antonio, TX 78217
(210) 348-7375

Key Texas Parks and Wildlife Website Links

Home Page .... tpwd.texas.gov/
Wildlife Div....... tpwd.texas.gov/about/administration-divisions/wildlife
Licenses........... tpwd.texas.gov/regulations/outdoor-annual/licenses/hunting-licenses-and-permits/hunting-licenses
Desert Sheep ... tpwd.texas.gov/regulations/outdoor-annual/regs/animals/desert-bighorn-sheep
Hunting Regs....tpwd.texas.gov/documents/237/pwd_bk_l2000_1170a.pdf

Texas Sheep Hunting Overview
(2023-2024)

Texas has worked diligently to restore its desert sheep populations in the western part of the state over the last 50 years or so, and wildlife officials are careful with the annual permit-tags for these animals. Typically, only about 20 desert bighorn sheep permits are available each year. Two are available through a raffle or public drawing, and another is auctioned off by a nonprofit chosen by Texas Parks and Wildlife. The remaining permits are issued to private landowners, which has been my own experience on sheep hunts in Texas.

All of these hunts are in West Texas, and permit competition is pretty fierce. The public draw tag for the 2022-2023 season saw 6,491 applicants pay the $10 app fee for this single permit. The lucky winner got a five-day guided hunt with food, lodging and transportation provided. Harvest success on these annual public draw permits is nearly 100 percent.

Most bighorn sheep hunters in Texas buy their permits from landowners, and these coveted tags can be pretty pricey. Permits are allocated based on availability of surplus desert bighorns. Landowners are encouraged to support management activities to aid bighorn on their lands. The income they receive selling these permits is likely encouragement enough. In 2024, the department's website did not list landowners with sheep permits. Most of the outfitters for sheep hunts in West Texas know the landowners with permits—which are rumored to sell at around $80,000 of late.

Application date for 2024 for both the permit draw and the Big Time Texas Hunts raffle was October 15, 2023. Seasons for hunting desert bighorns in Texas may be best obtained by talking with a state wildlife official. The department's website provided little guidance for sheep hunting season.

Hunting regulations can be downloaded in PDF format to your home computer with the Summary of Hunting Regulations link above. This publication was not as comprehensive as most other sheep-hunting states' regulations booklet. Texas seemed to prefer

184

putting more of their hunting information online.

General hunting licenses are $25 for residents and $315 for non-residents. The general hunting license is required for non-residents to hunt bighorn sheep in Texas. Licenses can be purchased online or through hundreds of retailers throughout the state.

Success rates on the few bighorn hunts are said to be high, although the Texas Parks and Wildlife website has little information on this. Harvest information in Texas may be available for prior years by emailing the department at: hunt@tpwd.texas.gov.

Skirting the southern boundaries of Big Bend National Park, the steep rocky banks along the slow-moving waters of the Rio Grande provide an excellent habitat for some of the Texas desert bighorns.

UTAH
Licensing and Permitting

Utah Division of Wildlife Resources Home Page: wildlife.utah.gov
1549 W. North Temple
Salt Lake City, UT 84116
(801) 538-4700

OFFICE LOCATIONS

CENTRAL REGION
1115 N. Main Street
Springville, UT 84663
(435) 781-9453

SOUTHEASTERN REGION
319 N. Carbonville Rd, Ste. A
Price, UT 84501
(435) 613-3700

SOUTHERN REGION
1470 N. Airport Road
Cedar City, UT 84721
(435) 865-6100

Key Utah Division of Wildlife Resources Website Links

Home Page .... wildlife.utah.gov
Main Hunting Page .... wildlife.utah.gov/hunting/main-hunting-page.html
Big Game App Guide ... wildlife.utah.gov/guidebooks/biggameapp.pdf
Big Game Regs Guide .... wildlife.utah.gov/guidebooks/field_regs.pdf
Hunter Education .... wildlife.utah.gov/hunting/hunter-education.html
Map of Hunt Areas .... dwrapps.utah.gov/huntboundary/
Permit Draw Results .... utah-hunt.com/UT_Returncard/?AspxAutoDetectCookieSupport=1
Hunt Tables & Maps .... wildlife.utah.gov/hunting/maps.html

Utah Sheep Hunting Overview
(2023-2024)

Utah's desert sheep population has been growing over the decades with an upward trend of increasing numbers of permits since 1993. The Division of Wildlife Resources website provided good guidance in 2024 for sheep hunters. The Big Game Application Guidebook and Big Game Field Regulations Guidebook (links to both above) could be downloaded for ongoing reference.

Online applications for big game hunt permits (which included desert sheep hunts) began on March 21 in 2024 and ran through April 25. Drawing results were available by May 16. Permits were mailed to draw winners in early July. Permit applicants were required to have valid hunting/combo licenses. Those born after Dec. 31, 1965, were required to provide proof of having passed a hunter education course before applying for licenses and permits (see Hunter Ed link above).

Residents age 18-64 in 2024 paid $44 for a 365-day combination license; residents 65 and older paid $35. Non-residents 18 and over paid $150 for a 365-day combination license. Draw applicants also paid a non-refundable app fee of $10 for residents and $16 for non-residents. Permit fees for a desert bighorn were $564 for residents and $2,244 for non-residents. Permit fees are not charged until an applicant is drawn.

Bonus points for future draws can be accumulated by those not

---

2024 Desert Bighorn Draw Results in Utah

Residents		Non-Residents	
Permits	Applicants	Permits	Applicants
69	8,660	5	12,707

2022 Desert Bighorn Harvest Summary in Utah

Harvest	Hunters	% Successful
75	80	93.8

---

drawn for a permit. Utah is another "one-and-done" state for sheep hunters.

In 2024, the division's Hunt Tables and Maps link (see above) opened to a page with another link titled "Desert bighorn sheep." This link provided a wealth of online maps of sheep hunting areas, estimates of sheep in the various areas, a drawing odds report, population estimates of sheep in the various areas, and annual harvest reports. This was a comprehensive, sophisticated online service that anyone who hunts sheep in Utah could appreciate.

Desert ram season on open units for those with sportsman permits ran from Aug. 31 through Dec. 31, 2024. Sportsman permits, however, are for Utah residents only. Non-residents apply for permits by hunt number in designated areas. The desert bighorn season in most of the 17 designated areas ran from Sept. 14 to Nov. 10. Two of the areas ran later in the year.

Sheep Hunting in Mexico

U.S. outfitters are almost always your best source of information for hunting sheep in Mexico. I strongly recommend you find a U.S. outfitter who supports hunts in Mexico. As clearly as I can state it: *Don't even think about crossing the border without having an outfitter to guide you through the rules and regulations of hunting south of the U.S. border.*

You'll be especially dependent on your outfitter on these Mexican hunts. Besides the language barrier with Mexican officials, Mexican wildlife departments just don't have the resources to aid sheep hunters. So take extra care to get an outfitter you can work with.

Final Thoughts

While not comprehensive, I hope this chapter provides enough information to get you on your way to planning your sheep hunt. If you are averse to using websites, I advise you to find a son, daughter or friend who can help you fight through the various states' online application processes and their rules and regulations.

I also advise you to download, store and print out the publications on hunting regulations and application guidelines, which are on nearly all of these states' website. These publications are usually in a PDF (portable document format) that can be easily downloaded. Once printed to hard copy, you can highlight or underline key information, file these pages, and use them for repeated references. This sure beats running back to you computer over and over every time a new question arises.

When all else fails in your search for guidance, you can call a wildlife official in the state where you plan to hunt (relevant phone numbers conveniently listed above). Hint: you'll probably have to make a phone call or two no matter how web-savvy you may be. By the way, these state wildlife officials can provide key information on which hunting units have the most accessible sheep and on your chances of drawing a permit-tag. Your best data on sheep may come from one of the wildlife biologists, who are often surprisingly helpful.

Before you go into the mechanics of obtaining a permit and following the rules to hunt desert sheep, I want to call your attention to several other considerations related to this outdoor quest. Chief among these is your own attitude. Hunting desert sheep is difficult and requires some real "fire in the belly" to be consistently successful—or maybe successful even once. You'll be physically tested, and you'll have to maintain a positive attitude to pass that test. You can't let those steep slopes and rocky ridges dissuade you from pursuing that prize ram. You've got to be that "little engine that could."

It will be much easier to be that "little engine" if you are physically fit before going into a hunt. "Fatigue makes cowards of us all," Gen. George Patton warned his troops—an admonition later passed on by Green Bay Packers coach Vince Lombardi to his players. I have seen a wannabe sheep hunter give up on his first day in the field after being guided to the base of some formidable mountainside. After one look at those steep slopes on a windy, overcast day, he just decided this might not be something he wanted to tackle.

Now, if this soft-looking hunter had prepared himself with a good fitness program before booking that hunt, he might have seen those slopes more as a challenge to overcome rather than a good reason to call the whole thing off. In a big way, the fire in the belly of the little engine that could is stoked by aerobic exercise and strength training.

In Appendix 1, I offer some ideas on how to better ensure that you are physically prepared for one of these rigorous outdoor adventures.

Besides being physically fit, another big consideration for sheep hunters is their field gear. Having the proper gear goes beyond being armed with a good rifle and the ability to use it. If you're not getting a good night's rest or your feet are killing you when hiking on rocky terrain, you can rapidly lose interest in obtaining that prized sheep mount. In Appendix 2, you'll find a list of important gear every desert sheep hunter should consider before taking the field. This is largely based on my considerable experience on these hunts.

Good luck and good hunting!

The author with his display of some of his sheep mounts from a decade of hunting wild sheep in North America.

APPENDIX 1

Weekly Training for Desert Sheep Hunting

If you aren't physically and mentally prepared for a desert sheep hunt, you shouldn't plan on going. If you are unfit, there are few things more intimidating than standing at the base of a mountain—a really big mountain—and thinking, "I've got to climb that?"

Here's my weekly physical training program to prepare you for that mountain. Endurance is everything!

Monday/Wednesday/Friday

Morning Workout (upper body):
- Lat pull down (3 sets of 20)
- Triceps bench curls, alternating arms (3 sets of 20)
- Bench set-ups extension (6 sets of 20)
- Bench press (3 sets of 20)
- Seated bicep curls, alternating arms (3 sets of 20)
- One-arm dumbbell row (3 sets of 20)
- Ab pull-downs (3 sets of 20)
- Standing, one-arm triceps extensions, alternating arms (3 sets of 20)
- One-arm side extensions, very light weight (3 sets of 20)
- Handshake extension (3 sets of 20)
- Cable curls (3 sets of 20)
- Standing upright rows, 3 sets of 20
- Incline bench set-ups: (3 sets of 10), (set of 10 at 45 degrees), (set of 10 at 45-degree w/dumbbell bench press)
- Incline extension kick-out
  (Workout should be completed in 90 minutes)

Evening Workout (legs):
- Monday (5-mile run/walk) or 45 minutes on Stairmaster with boots and backpack
- Wednesday (5-mile run/walk or long bicycle ride)
- Friday (yoga in the evening)

Weekly Training for Desert Sheep Hunting
(continued)

Tuesday/Thursday

Morning workout (lower body & legs):
- Step Up (3 sets of 12; work up to 25 lbs. in each hand)
- Lunges without weight (3 sets of 20 long steps; work up to 25 lbs. in each hand)
- Leg press (20 reps; build up to heavy weights)
- Leg curl machine (3 sets of 20)
- Mule kicks (3 sets of 20; begin on cables, do not go heavy, work up slowly to avoid hamstring cramps)
- Abductor, exterior and interior (3 sets of 20 reps; careful to avoid muscle pull)

Evening workout (legs):
- Tuesday, 25-mile bike ride
- Thursday, 23-mile bike ride on hills

Saturday:
- Bike ride of approximately 45 miles with a one- to three-mile walk
- Grill out and drink beer

Sunday:
- Five- to 10-mile run/walk

For best conditioning, do this weekly workout for the three months prior to the mountain hunt. Adopt a kick-butt attitude on the hills when hunting. Get fit and don't be intimidated by the mountains and hikes. It's only walking, one step at a time. If you're fit, just remember: "If you think you can, you can!"

APPENDIX 2

Gear Requirements for Desert Sheep Hunting

Backpacks:
• external-frame backpack for trail hiking
• internal-frame backpack with compression straps for off-trail hiking (All backpacks should have deep cargo bay with side pockets and rifle or bow strap to free both hands.)
• pack cover

Basic Needs:
• rifle, ammunition, wind meter
• rain gear (A must! If you don't have it, don't go.)
• space blanket
• trekking poles
• ground cloth
• fire starter
• lighter (one in all pants or jacket pockets)
• (2) LED headlamp (miner's light) with extra batteries
• emergency light (Just break it and it's on.)
• chlorine tablets to purify water (depending on area)
• extra pair of socks
• wind stopper and balaclava head gear (use as a head or neck cover)
• five foot of quarter-inch rope
• light and heavy gloves
• beanie or cap
• knives (skinning and caping)
• bear spray
• survival kit
• field wipes
• signal safety light
(continued on next page)

Basic Needs for Backpack Hunt (additional to previous):
- quality, light-weight sleeping bag (KUIU 00 bag for cold weather)
- sleeping pad
- top-of-line, one-man tent
- light-weight butane stove with extra butane container
- high-carbohydrate food
- daypack
- light-weight, water resistant clothing with wicking action (quick-drying; warm even when wet)
- quality hiking boots
- binoculars
- range finder
- camera and/or camcorder
- sunscreen
- solar charger for cell or satellite phone
- backpack towel
- notebook and pen
- "victory cigar" (several)

About the Author

Oklahoma-based commercial developer, hunter and outdoorsman Leonard Hansen achieved a Double Grand Slam of North American wild sheep in 2014 and has taken all four of the sub-species of desert bighorn rams while hunting in southwestern United States and northwestern Mexico.

A longtime board member of the Oklahoma City chapter of Safari Club International, Hansen had pursued deer, antelope, elk and moose before setting his sights on wild sheep. It was while hunting mule deer outside the East Gate of Yellowstone National Park that he first got a good view this iconic game trophy and became intrigued with its pursuit.

To share the memories, excitement and experience of his adventures hunting desert bighorn sheep, the hunter has authored his latest book. He provided a previous work on hunting a variety of big game, *North American Mountain Hunting,* and an earlier account of his eight-year struggle for his first Grand Slam of North American bighorn sheep, *The Great Wild Sheep Adventure.*

Autographed copies of *North American Desert Sheep Hunting, North American Mountain Hunting,* and *The Great Wild Sheep Adventure* can be ordered directly at:

oklahomabooksonline.com/leonard-hansen

Other Books by the Author

Leonard Hansen eventually became smitten with wild sheep fever, but not before decades of notable outdoor adventures hunting deer, elk, moose, mountain goat and grizzly bear throughout the United States and Canada. *North American Mountain Hunting* takes the reader along on these varied and challenging game hunts.

The Great Wild Sheep Adventure chronicles Hansen's first Grand Slam of North American wild sheep. The narrative follows the lessons this already-seasoned hunter learned while pursuing these iconic trophy rams in their rugged, inaccessible habitat from Alaska to the Rio Grande.

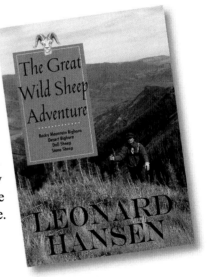

Autographed copies can be purchased at:
oklahomabooksonline.com/leonard-hansen

Made in the USA
Monee, IL
19 November 2024

8a61ce53-393e-40d4-a8d6-e1947efecb30R01